The World's Greatest Speeches

Jasvinder Kaur

Lotus PRESS
4735/22, Prakash Deep Building
Ansari Road, Darya Ganj,
New Delhi - 110002

Lotus Press : Publishers & Distributors
Unit No. 220, 2nd Floor, 4735/22, Prakash Deep Building,
Ansari Road, Darya Ganj, New Delhi- 110002
Ph.: 41325510, 98118-38000
• E-mail : lotuspress1984@gmail.com
www.lotuspress.co.in

The World's Greatest Speeches

ISBN: 81-8382-129-4

Printed & Published by : **Lotus Press Publishers & Distributors,** New Delhi-02

The World's Greatest Speeches

Published by :
Lotus Press Publishers & Distributors

PREFACE

The art of public speaking or speech requires a nice blend of a good write up and a way of presenting it that might make the audience stand on their feet to applaud. It has the opinion of the speaker presented in a manner and mode that captivates the audience from the start to the end.

Good and inspiring speeches have played an interesting part in history, encouraging people to do accomplish great tasks. Whether talking about a soliloquy in a Shakespearean play or Martin Luther King's 'Have a Dream' speech, their effect on the audience is incalculable. What made them so very popular is not just their text, but also the way in which they were delivered.

Speakers need to be conscious about their body language and their voice modulation. Starters often get nervous the moment they step on the stage. Here is a guide to delivering a speech that would prove to be helpful not just in writing one, but would also enrich the readers with tips on delivering it in such a way that would leave an indelible impression on the minds of the listeners.

A collection of memorable speeches from the past adds perfection to the book and makes it a sure guide to achieving success in learning the tricks of making a good speech.

Author

CONTENTS

1

Introduction to Speeches

For many people, the prospect of writing a speech and delivering it in front of a large group of audience is always frightening. However, if you're armed with an enthralling informative speech, it will end up being a pleasurable experience instead of a frightening one.

It all starts with an enticing start. The first twenty seconds can make or break you. If your speech starts off dull, your audience will not be captivated, feeling as if you had spruced their energy level in the beginning, even if your speech progresses with recitement. If your topic matter allows it, open with a funny or absurd joke. If it is more serious, such as a famous historical figure, ask a thought provoking question as an opening statement. Just try to get their attention.

Perhaps starting off with a simple 'Hi', and then a thoughtful pause works wonders. Silence is a wonderful tool for tricking your audience into paying attention. Once they are listening, then you can approach them, as a friend and explain what you are going to talk about. So your very first few sentences should be ravishing, exciting, or very subdued... then change your tenor completely and tell them what you want them to learn through your speech, and how you plan to explain it.

This does not have to be a tedious procedure. For example, let's say you want to tell them about Joan of Arc. For the speech, you can start off with a two sentence quote, in her native language, *i.e.* French. Since the majority of the audience will not understand what you are saying, this will perk their interest. Next, go on about the atrocities which she encountered, and change voice tones, usurping their attention and creating a feeling of compassion in the room.

Once you have explained the subject matter, and they feel as if they are prepared for the oncoming speech, startle them by stepping off your soap box, and walking around the room, ask a few rhetorical questions, keep throwing them for a loop. Make sure to write in the pauses in your speech, and put notes telling yourself when to smile, when to frown, and when to walk around. Continue with the subject matter, edit in facts, stories, quotations, and keep it a guessing game. Make it fun. Make sure that what you've written is not be something suitable for a book, yet something suitable for a dinner conversation. Even if the speech is for an advertising company, don't make it too formal, this will make the audience uncomfortable.

When you come near the end, put places in your speech for dramatic pauses, and wind down a bit to prepare the audience for the ending. The final few seconds of your speech should be more exciting and enthralling than the opening statements. Shock them, writing something which doesn't jive with your previous writing tone, make your speech one to remember. A speech should not be written in parts, instead block out a large chunk of time and simply write.

Hot Guiding Principles for an Astounding Speech

Before going to the stage for delivering a speech or before getting down on a table to write one, you need to have a strong groundwork to get started with. Have a quick look at these tips that are a sure shot guide to giving a memorable speech.

Know your Audience

This is the most important piece of advice–Never forget who

you're talking to. You're not speaking to a wall or your mother or your friends (even if all of these are in the crowd). You're speaking to a specific audience. And audiences, by definition, gather together to watch something that's worth their being held hostage in a cramped room for an extensive amount of time.

Do not fear from your audience. An audience is much easier to control than separate individuals. In order to woo your audience, you must do two things: find out what they want to hear, and figure out how to get that message across.

Know what the audience wants to hear. Each audience is different. Keeping this earth-shattering revelation in mind. Here's how to gear your speech towards a specific audience:

- Research your audience. Find out what the average audience member will be like. What will their average age be? What about their familiarity with the subject? Will they be fun loving or stodgy? What are they expecting to learn from you? Thinking about these simple elements will set you on the right track.
- Use appropriate words and body language. For example, career-day speech in an elementary school classroom is not the place to start pulling out terms like, 'Networking', 'Software Development', etc. when what is really needed to be said is, 'I work with computers'. But if you're giving a presentation to a group of programming colleagues, you should by all means refer to what you do as a 'Network Engineer', or a 'Software Developer'. The point is that if the audience doesn't understand your words, your speech will completely fly over their heads. If the words you use are too simple, your speech will be drowned out by the snoring.
- Think about the image you want to convey. When you're speaking to children, you want to smile a lot and look friendly and warm. When delivering a presentation to a

group of distinguished colleagues, you still want to be accessible, but you must also maintain an authoritative air.

The whole point of giving a speech is not just to make it through all your index cards, but to also communicate something to your audience. Consider these suggestions to help you out:

- Treat the audience as a single entity. One trick of the trade is to pretend that the audience is just one person. When there's only one person that you have to worry about, you feel more of a personal connection to him/her. Your speech will take a back seat to the fact that you want the person who's listening to you to really understand what you're saying. So, imagine that you're delivering your presentation to a fat, multi-headed creature.
- Don't forget to make an eye contact. Nothing makes an audience more alert than a speaker who can stare down a crowd. Making eye contact means making a connection, and that is your number one goal. So, let your eyes wander up from your notes as often and naturally as possible.
- Consider letting the audience participate. It's not applicable to all speeches, but letting members of the audience participate during your presentation will warm up a crowd. It'll encourage them to pay attention, thus making you easier to understand. Participation can range anywhere from asking for a show of hands to dividing the group into little clusters and giving each cluster a task. However, you should never call on someone who is not prepared to answer, nor should you ever embarrass anybody (even if they deserve it).

Organise your Speech

Writing a strong speech can be complicated and one of the toughest tasks if you are not sure what you want to tell your audience and how. You need to organise your speech properly. Most speeches have three main components:

- Introduction
- Body
- Closing

The Introduction

This is possibly the most important part of your speech, because you want to grab your audience's attention from the start. So, come up with something clever, shocking, or interesting right at the very beginning. Here are some possible techniques to use:

- *Be dramatic.* In a slightly comic tone, say something like, "I'm about to reveal a plan that will drastically alter the face of humanity as we know it!" when your presentation is really about a new brand of facial soap.
- *Crack a joke.* Getting people to laugh will loosen them up and make them feel inclined to like you and hear what you have to say. Don't try this if your jokes are usually met by silence or groans. Test your opening out first on your most brutally honest friends.
- *Narrate a story.* This will make the audience see you as a person instead of a boring public speaker, thus giving you an air of accessibility. However, keep two things in mind while opening your speech with a story. Keep it short (under a minute) and keep it relevant to the rest of your presentation. The point of the story is to lead the audience into your speech, so if your anecdote ends with your dog saving the day, and your speech is about bank mergers, you might have a hard time segueing from the intro into the rest of the speech.
- *Put up a question.* Asking the audience for their input will make them feel involved. This works even if you're going to answer your own question.

The Body

The body is your actual speech. Everything you want to say should come out here in an organised and extensive fashion. Here are some possible techniques:

- Use a formal outline. You can prepare for writing the content of your speech by outlining your major points with those numerals. Most good speeches have two or three main points, each of which has a couple of sub-points or examples.

  Formally outlining your speech will make sure that your logical flow makes sense and that your audience doesn't get lost. It will also help you figure out where the holes in your speech are, in case you have to do some last minute extra research.

- Mind-mapping, technique developed by a British brain researcher in the 1970s, is a less stiff version of writing up an outline. Instead of making a list, you write the main topic of your speech in the centre of a piece of paper, and draw branches extending from it that highlight your key points. Then draw more branches from the key points to elaborate on the sub-points.

  The good thing about mind maps is that they don't confine you to listing your ideas in any particular order; you can just use your creative juices and let the ideas flow. Then, once you've mind-mapped, you can create a more formal outline.

Always keep in mind that while writing down the body of the speech, you have to be organised. The audience must be able to follow your thoughts.

The Closing

The way you end a speech is almost as important as the way you begin it. The audience will be most restless at the end, and you have to find a way to tie everything together so that they don't walk away remembering how badly they were fidgeting. So, sum up everything for them in approximately a few concise sentences and leave them with a witty line.

If appropriate, you should also ask for questions. This doesn't mean saying, "Any- questions?-No?-I-didn't-think-so," and then running away. Instead, after you ask for questions, give the audience at least 10 seconds to respond. If there are questions, keep each response short (under a minute), and never take a guess at an answer. If you don't know how to respond to something, take down the questioner's e-mail or phone number, and tell the person you'll get back to them soon. Or you could just say, "Honestly, I don't know," and leave it at that.

While Writing the Speech

Writing a good speech is something that people write entire books on. But here are some quick notes to consider:

- Vary your word choice. Your speech will get very boring very quickly if you repeatedly use the same words. So, use interesting and different words and phrases and keep things new.
- Get a thesaurus. All great writers use one to bring variety in the chain of words they use. However, while using a thesaurus, keep one thing in mind–use only those words that people know.
- Keep the writing conversational, no matter how technical or unexciting the subject content might be. No one likes being lectured at, so there are a couple tricks you can use to make it feel like a normal dinner table conversation.
- Throw out rhetorical questions as if you really expect answers, and you might even get nods of agreement.
- Incorporate words that you usually use while speaking, but not in writing, such as 'okay' (as in 'Okay, so we're all caught up...') or 'see' (as in 'See, the reason is...').

- Refer to the event. If you're speaking at a graduation, refer to the graduation. It makes your speech sound more personalised.
- Whenever possible, describe a feeling or situation in detail. The audience will follow you more easily if you paint a picture for them instead of continually throwing out dry, emotionless words. One way to do this is to use action verbs. For example, instead of saying, 'learn', try, 'elucidate'.
- Imagery can be very effective. For example, instead of telling little kids that bears have furs to protect them from cold, try saying:

"Imagine, one chilly night you get up and find yourself in Iceland. Hey, what a chilly thought???? You are shivering from cold and want to get back to your cosy bed somehow. You don't have anyone around to help you out, and suddenly you see Balu of Jungle Book sleeping next to you. What do you do? He's a friendly bear and you simply nudge your head into its belly. What a relief man!!! He's warm, cosy.... just like your bed. His body has lots of fur that keep him warm, and now you are getting that warmth as well...."

- Remember that humour almost always helps. It's even appropriate at eulogies. The essence is in the timing, though. It's a good idea to test humour out on friends prior to the actual presentation. Just in case it turns out that you're an unbelievably corny person. Leave out any humour that is even remotely offensive. Often, self-deprecating humour (that doesn't completely destroy your credibility as a speaker) works well.
- Rewrite your speech a number of times. Even the most brilliant writer never gets it perfect on the first try. So, you have to continually rewrite and tighten your speech. Get rid of superfluous information (no matter how funny it is), and make sure that each line has a point.
- After you've written your speech, it can be helpful to put it

on 3 x 5 index cards. They are easier to carry around and shuffle through, and because you don't want to spend your entire presentation reading (and not speaking), index cards will make you feel more inclined to glance up when you flip through them. Just be sure to put huge numbers on the front of each card, in case they accidentally get shuffled around. But don't use the index cards as a crutch, as then the audience might just think that you're talking to your hand.

- Theme reinforcers are simply the points that a speechwriter uses throughout his or her speech to 'reinforce' the central idea they are trying to get across. In Winston Churchill's famous commencement address to Westminster College in 1946, he emphasises over and over again on the need for cooperation against tyranny and war. His speech covered serious problems which the post-war world faced, including what he termed as the 'iron curtain' that had descended across the European continent. Many say that this speech was the beginning of the 'cold war'. What we can learn from his address is the importance of continually reiterating one idea. The effect that this speech had on the world is almost incalculable.
- Speechwriting is all about knowing your audience and addressing their concerns. Leave your audience with something about which to think. Include humour and inspirational quotes. But make sure that all of them are integrated into the whole. Study the great speeches of the past to find inspiration. The joy that you will feel when you have given a speech that has inspired people is amazing and worth the effort.

Practice Correctly

Every good speaker needs to rehearse his/her speech several times before presenting it. The best speakers become effective speakers through constant practice. The main things to keep in mind are Method of Practice, Gestures, Voice Projection, and Visual Aids (when necessary).

Methods of Practice

There are several methods of practicing speech. Have a look at some common methods.

Mirror Practice

Stand in front of a full-length mirror and try to look like a public speaker. Keep your posture straight, your hands in sight, and look into your own eyes. Tell yourself, "Gosh, people want to hear what I have to say!" and then begin delivering your speech. Be conscious of the way you look in the mirror and adjust yourself accordingly as you're talking. Make sure that you're not being stiff, but always maintain an alert posture, or the audience will end up imitating your slump. Look into your eyes whenever you look up from your notes, and look up from your notes often.

Recording the Act

Tape record or (even better) videotape yourself delivering the presentation. When you replay the tape, listen to determine if everything sounds coherent and logical, and watch the way you look while speaking. Look for eye contact, gestures, and weird facial tics.

Demo Session

Gather together some friends, family, and pets, sit them down, and deliver your whole speech to them. After it's over, ask them to give you some constructive feedback (the last thing you need to do is have your confidence shaken). Ask them to tell you about what you did well and what you need to work on. Ask them to tell you what they didn't understand. If they have no advice to offer, tell them that if you bomb during the real thing, they'll have to eat the rotten tomatoes sliding down your body.

Mini-Rehearsals

Rehearse small sections of your speech throughout the day. If you've got 5 or 10 minutes when you are free, go over parts of the speech in your mind. These mini-rehearsals are easier to fit into your schedule and will give you a chance to practice parts of the speech that are giving you trouble.

As you improve, see if you can memorise sections without relying on the notes at all. These memorised sections will give you prolonged time to connect to the audience. Once you feel very comfortable with the material, don't be afraid to ad-lib some parts when you feel like it. This is your speech and you can say whatever you want; as long as you're sure you can get back on track, try speaking off the cuff. It'll help you sound conversational instead of like a robot.

Incorporate Gestures

It is not fun to watch a Popsicle! It is imperative that you occasionally use a gesture or two during your speech. Here are some tips for effective gesturing:

- Remember that 'Less is More'. The more gestures you make, the more it takes away the power of each gesture. So, use gestures to emphasise important points. If you use too many gestures, you'll look like a windmill.
- Use gestures when using active words. So, if you're talking about a merger between two people (or organisations or concepts), use a gesture that emphasises it.
- Practice your gestures in front of the mirror as you rehearse.
- Finally, don't forget the most important gesture: to SMILE. It makes you look more comfortable and less like a victim in front of a firing squad.

Project your Voice

Contrary to popular belief, projecting your voice does not mean shouting. When you project, you simply raise the volume of your natural speaking voice without losing control of it (that's when it becomes 'shouting'). Think of the difference between talking to someone in a noisy restaurant, and calling your dog in from the backyard.

You must always project while giving a speech, even if you are presenting in a small room. Find the object furthest away from you and deliver your speech to it. During the first minute of speaking, monitor your audience members' faces (especially the ones in the back row) to see if they look confused. If you notice that they are not paying attention from the very start, stop yourself and ask if everyone can hear you. If there's no reply, you just got your answer!

Use Visual Aids when Necessary

Visual aids are not always necessary, but they are good to include if they help you get your point across. The key is to make sure that they add to your speech and don't appear to have been added just for the sake of it. After all, it's just plain dumb if during a speech about saving the trees, you whip out a picture of a tree. We all know what trees look like. It is equally useless to present a very complicated diagram that someone sitting in the tenth row can barely see, let alone decipher. So, keep your visual aids/very simple. Images and uncomplicated graphs are best, but if you want to make a list of points to go over, keep each line of the list brief, and the number of lines just as short. Five words per line and five lines per visual aid are ideal.

Handle Nervousness

Remind yourself–'It's just a speech'. Your life does not depend on it. However, if the thought of going out there and completely freezing up makes you freeze up go through some of these relaxing exercises just prior to your performance.

Physical Preparation

- The night before, don't eat dairy product or drink milk. They may cause you to phlegm up. Also, no soda, coffee, tea, or other caffeinated drinks for at least an hour before the speech. They'll just make you even antsier.
- The morning of your speech, brush your teeth and use mouthwash. A clean mouth is a happy mouth.
- Look presentable. Dress in nice clothes, comb your hair, do your nails, and groom yourself so that you look as nice as possible. As the saying goes, "Dress to impress." The nicer you look, the more credibility you'll have with the audience.
- Go to the bathroom about a half-hour before the speech.
- Deep breathing exercises may seem cheesy, but they really slow your heart rate, lower your blood pressure, and reduce your adrenaline flow. So, try breathing in through your nose, holding your breath for five seconds, and breathing out through your mouth. Do this at least three times, but don't go over six, or you may either keel over or start to hyperventilate.
- If hand gestures are a part of your presentation, shake up your hands to get the blood going. This exercise will make it more natural for you to move them around during the performance.
- Vocal exercises can help. Prepare your mouth by running through your speech at full voice several times. If you screw up, just keep remembering that the audience won't have a text and see where you screw up. Just move on as if nothing happened.
- Most importantly, "Be Confident!" Even if you're not, the

better you fake it, the more comfortable the audience will be with you, and thus, the more positive vibes they'll throw your way.

Mental Preparation

- Think these comforting thoughts (and true facts) before and during your presentation:

"The audience's initial impression of me is made within the first three seconds of my appearance." This can be used to your advantage because if you make sure you walk onto the stage with a bright smile and confident posture, you already have it made.

"I look better than I feel." Everyone feels like a wreck when they first get up there, but most don't look like one. In fact, most people who videotape themselves giving a rehearsal presentation are pleasantly surprised to find out that their wildly beating heart actually doesn't show up on the tape.

"The audience wants me to succeed!" An audience is made up of people who are not unlike you. They are not bloodthirsty animals and their shoes are too valuable to toss at you. They came to hear you because you have something important to say. Also, because they don't want their time to be wasted, it's in their best interest for you to succeed.

"A mistake will not matter much." Granted, people won't forget a nasty belch in the middle of a serious point, but completely ignore stumbles or slight pauses. Just move on. Most people won't notice your mistakes unless you draw attention to them by panicking.

Dealing with Presentation Disasters

Most presentation disasters are not fatal. They can be resolved comfortably if you keep certain rules close at hand, in your mind. Know exactly what you want the decision maker to do.

Here are some of the conventional situations when the speaker finds himself in troubled waters.

The decision maker is forced to leave before you have gotten to your key points.

If you follow the old rule, "Tell them what you are going to tell them, tell them, tell them what you told them," you won't get caught this way. Always mention your main point and major supporting points within the first few minutes of any presentation. If you are using visuals, you always have a visual that has the main point and the key points. If, however, you have made the fatal error of trying to save the 'zinger' for last, and the decision maker must leave, ask for a moment to summarise (anyone will give you a moment if you ask with a smile) and state, in one sentence, the one point you want the decision maker to remember and, if you have a chance, the two concepts that best support that point.

You arrive and are told the decision maker can't attend.

Even if the decision maker can't make it, someone in the room will be responsible for reporting to him or her. Ask yourself, "What, in one sentence, do I want the reporter to say?" (What do I want the decision maker to do?). Then, be sure you state that sentence, as you want it repeated, at the beginning and at the end of your presentation.

You find you have far less time than you had planned on.

Talking fast never works. Decide quickly what percentage of the time you have each part of your presentation should take. Keep your eye on your watch and limit yourself to the key concept in each portion. Next time, be prepared. Think about what you'll leave out if your time is halved.

You are asked a question you plan to discuss in detail later.

Answer the question briefly, and say you plan to go into detail later. If person asking the question is the decision maker, ask if the short answer is sufficient for now. Do not ask people to wait until you reach the point at which you originally planned to cover the material. If you do, everyone will focus on the unanswered question instead of listening. And, in a meeting setting, do not ask people to hold their questions until the end. Making that request suggests you are not confident enough to deal with interruptions.

You lose your train of thought mid-sentence.

Smile, say, "Excuse me!" and start it again. Keep in mind that everyone in the room has lost track of an idea at least once. People want you to succeed and are sympathetic. Keep smiling.

You plan to work through a handout pagewise but people are moving at their own pace.

The risk in giving people printed material is that they will read it at their own pace. If at all possible, don't provide handouts until after the presentation is over. If you must walk through a printed booklet, tell people what it contains and give them a rough idea of where different parts are located before you begin. If possible, hold your copy up as an easel and point to parts of charts or graphs. People are also more likely to stay with you if you occasionally say, "And you can see on page ___ that..." If the decision maker insists on moving ahead quickly, you'll do best to pick up the pace, perhaps skip pages, and, if necessary, focus on the pages that are important to them.

You expect to speak to 3 people and arrive to find 20.

If you were planning to work from one set of handouts, forget it. Ask for a flipchart and pens; decide quickly how much you can rough sketch as you talk (key points, if nothing else). Stand; it is easier to maintain control. Remember that you are the expert. Keep smiling.

Your throat dries out.

Do what the theatre folk do. Roll a tiny piece of paper into a small ball and place it between your gum and your facial tissue in the back of your mouth. It will stimulate the flow of saliva just like the wad of cotton the dentist uses. Try this in private first, however, so that you are sure you are comfortable.

Several people start a side conversation while you are speaking.

In the following order: Ask if there are questions. Ask if you can do anything to clarify. If they will not stop and you are standing, continue your presentation but try to move nearer to them. Lower your voice or pause. Hope that someone else will stop them. When all else fails, try to acknowledge that things are out of control and ask the group whether a new meeting should be scheduled.

You drop your overheads on the floor.

Make a joke about your clumsiness, pick them up and take a few moments to put them in order. (Now is the time to be grateful you have numbered them.)

What to do when you forget something?

You're flowing smoothly through your presentation and all of a sudden you go blank. There's nothing upstairs. Nothing on-line. You lick your lips, clear your throat, and say "uh". Your eyes begin to dart about in desperation, and as the internal pressure mounts, the real signals of distress pour out: giggling, blushing, and embarrassing true confessions of just how lost you really are, revealing only your lack of preparation and diminished professionalism.

But, this no way is the end of the world. Here's how to deal with it:

- First, use an ounce of prevention. Rehearse out loud

frequently enough to internalise your message. Strangely, if you try to memorise your remarks, you're almost sure to go blank. Understand why you're speaking the words you choose, and say them in rehearsal until you have a gut feeling for the essence of your message.

- Use your visuals as a road map, if possible. Using graphic images or bullet points, rely on your visuals to keep you on track. Visuals should not serve as a script, but rather as a series of trigger points that generate discourse.
- Keep your notes nearby. Make sure they're written in large, colourful writing. They'll be easy to read when you're under pressure.
- Focus your eyes on one person in the audience when you go blank. They'll think you're being forceful and dramatic. Then, after about four seconds, move your eyes to another person. Do it again. Keep doing this through the silence until your brain comes back to life.
- Repeat what you just said. Using repetition is a good speaking technique anyway. Keep repeating yourself until your mind clicks into gear. Or say something that parallels your subject, and chances are, within seconds, you'll be back on track.
- Ask the audience a question if it's a small group. "Marilyn, what are your thoughts so far?" Make it an open-ended question so Marilyn can't say simply "yes" or "no." That way, you get more time to think as Marilyn speaks. If you're speaking to a large group, ask a rhetorical question. Again, you'll probably wake yourself up quickly.
- Ask for help. "Where was I?" is not a shameful thing to say. Most audiences will be sympathetic. Everyone knows the pressure of speaking. Just don't do it repeatedly or make a big deal out of it.

Setting the Speech

There are speakers who talk so fast that the audience is left in the dust. Listeners may end up ten words behind, especially if the topic is complex or unfamiliar. In sales, a rapid rate of speech can result in a lost potential sale.

People talk so fast because others around them do this, because they think erroneously that others will not take the time to listen to them, and because they do not realise the listeners are struggling. In some cultures, speaking quickly is a sign of professional competence.

In some countries, the average speech rate is 120-140 words per minute. It is faster in some places such as New York City, and slower in some others. What matters is not how many words a speaker can get out, but how many (well-chosen) words are understood by the listener.

Speech rate becomes a problem in any location when the listener does not understand. The speaker either may have to repeat himself, or some information gets ignored. In a healthcare setting, this can be a real danger as instructions may get confused and patient compliance may slip. Young children and senior citizens may also process information more slowly.

If you are a fast speaker, and you know this is a problem, start by listing the reasons you want to slow down. Maybe you want a promotion, but need clearer speech. Possibly your colleagues are getting frustrated with your speech. Perhaps you are tired of repeating yourself. Possibly phone calls are not returned because others cannot understand your telephone number or name.

Start by taking some slow, deep breaths. Then, count slowly to ten, prolonging the vowels if needed. Then say your ten digit telephone number at that slow rate. Visualise someone writing it down from a telephone message. Can he write it correctly at that pace?

Try saying some basic sentences at that slow pace, such as "I see a ______" or "_______ are great!" Then, slowly recite a shopping list. Can you slightly prolong the vowels? Other ways to think of it are to go at a 25 mph pace with your words, or visualise yourself rocking in a rocking chair, slowly talking. Often your listener will not even realise what you are doing.

Talk about a topic that is not important to you, such as a minor interest or a description of a person you casually noticed earlier. Speak at this more relaxed rate. Tape yourself if possible, and listen to it.

The real test comes when speaking about a topic that is important to you, such as family or work. Can you still maintain this slower rate, or at least use it when you notice the listener is confused?

Enlist some others to help you by discretely indicating when you are going too fast again. This may happen when making a presentation or when under other stress. Change does not happen overnight; be patient.

2

Language of the Body and Voice

Body language includes hand and arm gestures, facial expressions (including eye contact) and any other body movements. It is all non-verbal communication.

Body language in a speech serves 3 purposes:

- It illustrates and emphasises what you are saying in your speech.
- It makes a speech more interesting, *i.e.* it will assist in keeping the audience's attention.
- It helps release nervous energy which goes towards settling the nerves.

Actions speak louder than words

A research into communications showed that an audience is influenced by a speaker in the following percentages:

- Spoken Words 7%
- Voice 38%
- Body Language 55%

This clearly shows that:

- How you say the spoken words is important in order to get your message across and believed; but, even more important than that is your body language.
- An audience will be unimpressed if the speaker is not giving everything they've got *i.e.* with voice and body.

- A speaker's voice and body language should match the spoken word. He/she should be speaking with everything that he/she has got, like enthusiasm, passion, sincerity, and emotion, with both voice and body. For example, say out loud, "This is what I believe." First say it with no with passion, and a second time with passion in the voice and with fully body language, particularly with the use of arms and facial expressions. Feel the difference? The audience will be influenced very little on the words alone. They will be more influenced by the tone of what you say and the body language they see.
- It's important to use body language within your range of what is natural. If you want to expand the parameters of your range, exaggerate and be theatrical while speaking at a speaking club.
- If a speaker is speaking sincerely on a topic but standing stiffly without any body language, the audience will believe what they see and not think the speaker is sincere, and therefore, ignore the message.
- The body language should always match the words at the appropriate moment. The most difficult aspect is appearing natural when first incorporating body language into speeches. Rehearsing will help but don't worry if at first you have to force the body language to happen rather than it occurring naturally. Rehearsing in front of a mirror is a good idea.
- Keeping your **hands** by your side or resting them on the lectern will have them ready for action. This is better than having them in your pockets or clenched behind your back where they aren't in a position to be ready to start working.
- Avoid pacing, rocking, swaying, or leaning/slouching on the lectern, as this will be distracting to the audience, a sign of nerves and will prevent the upper body from using

body language. If the bottom half of the body is moving, the top half of the body (the important half) will not be able to spring into action naturally. Practice finding a stance that is comfortable. If it is comfortable for you then the audience will also find it comfortable. Except when you want to walk from one place to the other, keep from the hips down unwaveringly still. When you have increased your confidence from speaking in front of an audience several times, you will find that your hands, arms and body will start to move naturally. This is less likely to happen if there isn't a solid platform (i.e. bottom half of the body).

- Don't be afraid to make large, bold gestures. The larger the audience the larger gestures and body movement are needed in order to be effective.

Gestures

Gestures are the use of hands and arms to illustrate your words. There are four main groups of gestures.

Descriptive Gestures

These gestures are used to clarify or enhance. They help visualise size, weight, shape, location, function, direction, etc.

Emphatic Gestures

These are used when certain points are to be emphasised with great force. Here are some of the prominent emphatic gestures:

- Moving forward a clenched fist suggests strong feelings, such as anger or determination.
- Hitting your fist into your open palm shows importance or urgency.
- A folding of arms illustrates strength and determination.
- Clasping your hands together in front of your chest conveys unity.

- A forefinger pointed towards the ceiling means listen to me.
- You can show your clenched fist to urge action.

Suggestive Gestures

These are symbols of ideas or emotions.

- An open palm suggests giving or receiving.
- A shrug of the shoulders indicates ignorance, perplexity or irony.
- Comparison and contrast can be illustrated by either moving hands in unison or in opposite directions.

Prompting Gestures

These prompt or evoke a desired response from the audience. If you want your listeners to raise their hand, applaud or perform some action, you'll enhance the response by doing it yourself as an example.

Facial Expression

Your face communicates your attitude, feelings and emotions. Don't be scared to look angry, disappointed, or to smile, etc. In particular, smile. Smiling conveys warmth and sincerity and makes the audience more receptive to what you are saying.

Settling Nerves

Use your nervous energy, particularly at the start of your speech when you are more nervous, to make controlled body language. This is a better way than fidgeting with papers, adjusting items of clothing, pacing, etc. It will not be distracting for the audience and will help get your message across.

A Good Speaking Voice

In many cases, the speaker's voice does not completely captivate the audience, but it does have the potential to alienate them. Make sure that you don't underestimate the importance of your voice. Make sure that your audience can not only physically hear you, but will also want to physically hear you.

A good speaking voice should have the following attributes:

- The tone has a friendly, pleasant tone.
- It is natural, reflecting the true personality and sincerity of the speaker.
- It has life and vitality, even when it isn't very loud.
- It portrays various shades of meaning, never sounding monotonous or emotionless.
- It is easy to hear, thanks to good volume and clear articulation.

Principal Elements of Vocal Variety

The principal elements of vocal variety are Volume, Pace, Tone, Quality and Pause. A conversational style voice should be your base style from where you add variety.

Volume

Different levels of volume can be used as follows:

- *Loud* for emphasis, excitement, climax, punch-line, etc.
- *Normal* as the base level of your speech, *i.e.* conversational style which is adequate for the audience to hear but not overpowering.
- *Quiet* in case of conspiracy, secrecy, contrast, intimacy, etc.

Pace

Different levels of pace can be used as follows:

- *Fast* in case of excitement, fast action, etc.
- *Normal* as the base level of your speech, *i.e.* conversational style which is approximately 125–160 words per minute which ensures full pronunciation.

- *Slow* for contrast, clarity, relaxed, slow action, etc.

Tone (pitch)

The tone should reinforce the spoken words. Examples of different tones are assertive manner, friendly manner, pleading manner, questioning manner. You can use different pitches as follows:

- *High* for excitement, assertive, fear, etc.
- *Normal* for deeper voices and conversation style that are easier to listen to.
- *Low* in case of tiredness, slow action, boredom, etc.

Quality

Experience increases confidence which serves to improve the voice. Voice training exercises will improve the quality and pleasantness of your voice.

Pause

It can be the most deafening sound of all. Use it:

- Before and/ particularly after when emphasising something
- For a change of subject
- To imitate suspense before the punch line
- To give time for audience laughter

Some Exceptions

Speakers who have a naturally quiet voice may:

- Speak louder.
- Speak more often to increase confidence and strength.
- Speak in an assertive tone.
- Speak with lots of vocal variety.
- Carry out voice training exercises.

3

Common Speech Topics

College and school students are often required to give a speech. When the topic is given, the speakers get time to research and chose their material. This is fine, but the only disadvantage with this is that the speakers don't have the liberty to speak on their choice of subject.

The scenario is different, however, when the speakers are given the liberty to chose their topic and elaborate on it as per their will. This gives the speaker a chance to choose a subject that he/ she is very well familiar with and has something to say about it. This also goes as a guideline for starters to choose a topic that they are comfortable with and feel for it somewhere deep down.

Have a look at some of the important speech themes in different fields:

Persuasive Speech Topics

Abortion

Adoption

Affirmative Action Laws

Aliens and UFOs: Yes or No?

Animal Rights

Are there Angels among us?

Assisted Suicide

Bigamy

Birth Control

Books: Are they a thing of the Past?

Beauty is more than skin deep

Brand Names and Quality

Campus Issues - Dating

Campus Issues - Student Fees

Campus Issues - Student Life

Campus Issues - Technology

Capital Punishment

Censorship of Internet

Chat Rooms: Are they safe?

Cloning

Conservation and Recycling: Is it Important?

Cults Kill

Divorce: Does it destroy children?

Drunk Driving

Eating Less Meat

Feminism

Foreign Policy

Fur is not a Fashion Statement

Genetic Engineering

Global Warming: Fact or Fiction?

Government Regulation of Utilities

Human Cloning

Hunting Laws

Illiteracy: Is it a problem?

Immigrants and Illegal Aliens

Immunity Rights for Political Leaders

Mandatory Seatbelt Laws

Media Ethics

Medicare

Mothers should stay at home

Nuclear Weapons

Organ Transplants

Pesticide Use

Prayer in Schools

Smoking in Public Places

Space Programme

Terrorism

Test Tube Babies

Tobacco

Unemployment Compensation

School Speech Topics

Animal Life in Danger

Books

Business

Freedom Struggle

Healthy Eating

How much do we need to save for a comfortable life?

My dream holiday

My Pop Idol

Nature

On this day in history

Test marketing your idea

The first Moon Landing

The life and times of _____ (Mahatma Gandhi, Baba Sahib Ambedkar, Shaheed Bhagat Singh, etc.)

What I'd do if I won a lottery?

When will man get to Mars?

Who says that crime doesn't pay?

Controversial Speech Topics

Abortion

Birth Control

Discrimination Laws

Gene Testing

Human Cloning

Iraq War

Renewable Energy

Right of Privacy

Weapons of Mass Destruction

Informational Speech Topics

AIDS

Animal communication

Argumentation

Bad news delivery

Biography of an important person

Chemical warfare

Colour blindness

Communication in a classroom/office

Computer viruses

Conflict resolution strategies

Delivery styles

Electric and Alternative Fuel Vehicles

Family communication

Food preservatives

Gender differences in communication

Genetic cloning

Health communication

Intercultural communication

Just how long do we expect to live?

Mediation process

Personality tests

Political correctness

Political parties

Sibling rivalry

Stages of relationships

Top Internet searches

Types of relationships

What is inflation?

When will man get to Mars?

Argumentative/Debate Speech Topics

Abortion

AIDS education/awareness

Air Pollution

Assisted Suicide

Bioethics

Censorship

Cloning Research

College Athletics and Money

Computer Crimes
Computer Ethics
Corporal Punishment
Cyber Crime
Death Penalty
Ethics and Money, sport or business
Foreign Aid
Gay Rights
Genetic Testing
Gun Control
Human Rights
Hunting
Immigration
Intellectual Property and Piracy
Mandatory AIDS Testing
Mandatory Drug Testing
Mass Media and Privacy
Prostitution
Salaries of Professional Athletes
School Prayer
Smoking
Social Ethics
Surrogacy
Surrogate motherhood
Teen pregnancy

4

Some Memorable Speeches

Biographical Sketch: Abraham Lincoln (February 12, 1809–April 15, 1865) was the 16th President of the United States. He was a fierce opponent of the expansion of slavery. He helped preserve the United States by leading the defeat of the secessionist Confederacy in the American Civil War. He introduced measures that resulted in the abolition of slavery. His assassination in 1865 made him a martyr for the ideals of national unity.

Speeches By: Abraham Lincoln

Topic: The Gettysburg Address

Date: November 19, 1863 in Gettysburg, Pennsylvania

Four score and seven years ago our fathers brought forth on this continent, a new nation, conceived in Liberty, and dedicated to the proposition that all men are created equal.

Now we are engaged in a great civil war, testing whether that nation, or any nation so conceived and so dedicated, can long endure. We are met on a great battle-field of that war. We have come to dedicate a portion of that field, as a final resting place for those who here gave their lives that that nation might live. It is altogether fitting and proper that we should do this.

But, in a larger sense, we can not dedicate–we can not consecrate–we can not hallow–this ground. The brave men, living and dead, who struggled here, have consecrated it, far above our poor power to add or detract. The world will little note, nor long remember what we say here, but it can never forget what they did here. It is for us the living, rather, to be dedicated here to the unfinished work which they who fought here have thus far so nobly advanced. It is rather for us to be here dedicated to the great task remaining before us–that from these honored dead we take increased devotion to that cause for which they gave the last full measure of devotion–that we here highly resolve that these dead shall not have died in vain–that this nation, under God, shall have a new birth of freedom–and that government of the people, by the people, for the people, shall not perish from the earth.

★

Second Speech by: Abraham Lincoln

Topic: Last Public Address

Date: April 11, 1865 in Washington, D.C.

We meet this evening, not in sorrow, but in gladness of heart. The evacuation of Petersburg and Richmond, and the surrender of the principal insurgent army, give hope of a righteous and speedy peace whose joyous expression can not be restrained. In the midst of this, however, He from whom all blessings flow, must not be forgotten. A call for a national thanksgiving is being prepared, and will be duly promulgated. Nor must those whose harder part gives us the cause of rejoicing, be overlooked. Their honors must not be parcelled out with others. I myself was near the front, and had the high pleasure of transmitting much of the good news to you; but no part of the honor, for plan or execution, is mine. To General Grant, his skilful officers, and brave men, all belongs. The gallant Navy stood ready, but was not in reach to take active part.

By these recent successes the re-inauguration of the national authority–reconstruction–which has had a large share of thought from the first, is pressed much more closely upon our attention. It is fraught with great difficulty. Unlike a case of a war between independent nations, there is no authorized organ for us to treat with. No one man has authority to give up the rebellion for any other man. We simply must begin with, and mould from, disorganized and discordant elements. Nor is it a small additional embarrassment that we, the loyal people, differ among ourselves as to the mode, manner, and means of reconstruction.

As a general rule, I abstain from reading the reports of attacks upon myself, wishing not to be provoked by that to which I can not properly offer an answer. In spite of this precaution, however, it comes to my knowledge that I am much censured for some supposed agency in setting up, and seeking to sustain, the new State government of Louisiana. In this I have done just so much as, and no more than, the public knows. In the Annual Message of December 1863 and accompanying Proclamation, I presented a plan of re-construction (as the phrase goes) which, I promised, if adopted by any State, should be acceptable to, and sustained by, the Executive government of the nation. I distinctly stated that this was not the only plan which might possibly be acceptable; and I also distinctly protested that the Executive claimed no right to say when, or whether members should be admitted to seats in Congress from such States. This plan was, in advance, submitted to the then Cabinet, and distinctly approved by every member of it. One of them suggested that I should then, and in that connection, apply the Emancipation Proclamation to the theretofore excepted parts of Virginia and Louisiana; that I should drop the suggestion about apprenticeship for freed-people, and that I should omit the protest against my own power, in regard to the admission of members to Congress; but even he approved every part and parcel of the plan which has since been employed or touched by the action of Louisiana.

The new constitution of Louisiana, declaring emancipation for the whole State, practically applies the Proclamation to the part previously excepted. It does not adopt apprenticeship for freed-people; and it is silent, as it could not well be otherwise, about the admission of members to Congress. So that, as it applies to Louisiana, every member of the Cabinet fully approved the plan. The message went to Congress, and I received many commendations of the plan, written and verbal; and not a single objection to it, from any professed emancipationist, came to my knowledge, until after the news reached Washington that the people of Louisiana had begun to move in accordance with it. From about July 1862, I had corresponded with different persons, supposed to be interested, seeking a reconstruction of a State government for Louisiana. When the message of 1863, with the plan before mentioned, reached New-Orleans, General Banks wrote me that he was confident the people, with his military co-operation, would reconstruct, substantially on that plan. I wrote him, and some of them to try it; they tried it, and the result is known. Such only has been my agency in getting up the Louisiana government. As to sustaining it, my promise is out, as before stated. But, as bad promises are better broken than kept, I shall treat this as a bad promise, and break it, whenever I shall be convinced that keeping it is adverse to the public interest. But I have not yet been so convinced.

I have been shown a letter on this subject, supposed to be an able one, in which the writer expresses regret that my mind has not seemed to be definitely fixed on the question whether the seceding States, so called, are in the Union or out of it. It would perhaps, add astonishment to his regret, were he to learn that since I have found professed Union men endeavoring to make that question, I have purposely forborne any public expression upon it. As appears to me that question has not been, nor yet is, a practically material one, and that any discussion of it, while it thus remains practically immaterial, could have no effect other than the mischievous one of dividing our friends. As yet, whatever it may hereafter become, that question is bad, as the basis of a controversy, and good for nothing at all–a merely pernicious abstraction.

We all agree that the seceded States, so called, are out of their proper relation with the Union; and that the sole object of the government, civil and military, in regard to those States is to again get them into that proper practical relation. I believe it is not only possible, but in fact, easier to do this, without deciding, or even considering, whether these States have ever been out of the Union, than with it. Finding themselves safely at home, it would be utterly immaterial whether they had ever been abroad. Let us all join in doing the acts necessary to restoring the proper practical relations between these States and the Union; and each forever after, innocently indulge his own opinion whether, in doing the acts, he brought the States from without, into the Union, or only gave them proper assistance, they never having been out of it.

The amount of constituency, so to speak, on which the new Louisiana government rests, would be more satisfactory to all, if it contained fifty, thirty, or even twenty thousand, instead of only about twelve thousand, as it does. It is also unsatisfactory to some that the elective franchise is not given to the colored man. I would myself prefer that it were now conferred on the very intelligent, and on those who serve our cause as soldiers. Still the question is not whether the Louisiana government, as it stands, is quite all that is desirable. The question is, "Will it be wiser to take it as it is, and help to improve it; or to reject, and disperse it?" "Can Louisiana be brought into proper practical relation with the Union sooner by sustaining, or by discarding her new State government?"

Some twelve thousand voters[1] in the heretofore slave-state of Louisiana have sworn allegiance to the Union, assumed to be the rightful political power of the State, held elections, organized a State government, adopted a free-state constitution, giving the benefit of public schools equally to black and white, and empowering the Legislature to confer the elective franchise upon the colored man. Their Legislature has already voted to ratify the constitutional amendment recently passed by Congress, abolishing slavery throughout the nation. These twelve thousand persons are thus fully committed to the Union, and to perpetual freedom in the state–committed to the very things, and nearly all the things the nation wants–and they ask the nations recognition and it's assistance to make good their committal. Now, if we reject, and spurn them, we do our utmost to disorganize and disperse them. We in effect say to the white men, "You are worthless, or worse–we will neither help you, nor be helped by you." To the blacks we say, "This cup of liberty which these, your old masters, hold to your lips, we will dash from you, and leave you to the chances of gathering the spilled and scattered contents in some vague and undefined when, where, and how." If this course, discouraging and paralyzing both white and black, has any tendency to bring Louisiana into proper practical relations with the Union, I have, so far, been unable to perceive it. If, on the contrary, we recognize, and sustain the new government of Louisiana the converse of all this is made true. We encourage the hearts, and nerve the arms of the twelve thousand to adhere to their work, and argue for it, and proselyte for it, and fight for it, and feed it, and grow it, and ripen it to a complete success. The colored man too, in seeing all united for him, is inspired with vigilance, and energy, and daring, to the same end. Grant that he desires the elective franchise, will he not attain it sooner by saving the already advanced steps toward it, than by running backward over them? Concede that the new government of Louisiana is only to what it should be as the egg is to the fowl, we shall sooner have the fowl by hatching the egg than by smashing it? Again, if we reject Louisiana, we also reject one vote in favor of the proposed amendment to the national Constitution. To meet this proposition, it has been argued that no more than three fourths of those States which have not attempted secession are necessary to validly ratify the amendment. I do not commit myself against this, further than to say that such a ratification would be questionable, and sure to be persistently questioned; while a ratification by three-fourths of all the States would be unquestioned and unquestionable.

I repeat the question, "Can Louisiana be brought into proper practical relation with the Union sooner by sustaining or by discarding her new State Government?"

What has been said of Louisiana will apply generally to other States. And yet so great peculiarities pertain to each state, and such important and sudden changes occur in the same state; and withal, so new and unprecedented is the whole case, that no exclusive, and inflexible plan can be safely prescribed as to details and collaterals. Such exclusive, and inflexible plan, would surely become a new entanglement. Important principles may, and must, be inflexible.

In the present 'situation' as the phrase goes, it may be my duty to make some new announcement to the people of the South. I am considering, and shall not fail to act, when satisfied that action will be proper.

■

Biographical Sketch: Adolf Hitler (April 20, 1889–April 30, 1945) was Chancellor of Germany from 1933, and Führer (Leader) of Germany from 1934 until his death. He gained power when Germany was facing post World War I crisis. He appealed to the economic needs of the lower and middle classes using propaganda and charismatic oratory. His speeches sounded chords of nationalism, anti-semitism, and anti-communism. He restructured economy, rearmed military, and established a totalitarian regime. He pursued an aggressive foreign policy with the intention of expanding German Lebensraum ('living space'). This triggered World War II.

Speech By: Adolf Hitler

Topic: Speech of May 4, at Berlin, Reichstag

Date: May 4, 1941

Deputies. Men of the German Reichstag:

At a time when only deeds count and words are of little importance, it is not my intention to appear before you, the elected representatives of the German people, more often than absolutely necessary. The first time I spoke to you was at the outbreak of the war when, thanks to the Anglo-French conspiracy against peace, every attempt at an understanding with Poland, which otherwise would have been possible, had been frustrated.

The most unscrupulous men of the present time had, as they admit today, decided as early as 1936 to involve the Reich, which in its peaceful work of reconstruction was becoming too powerful for them, in a new and bloody war and, if possible, to destroy it. They had finally succeeded in finding a State that was prepared for their interests and aims, and that State was Poland.

All my endeavors to come to an understanding with Britain were wrecked by the determination of a small clique which, whether from motives of hate or for the sake of material gain, rejected every German proposal for an understanding due to their resolve, which they never concealed, to resort to war, whatever happened.

The man behind this fanatical and diabolical plan to bring about war at whatever cost was Mr. Churchill. His associates were the men who now form the British Government.

These endeavors received most powerful support, both openly and secretly, from the so-called great democracies on both sides of the Atlantic. At a time when the people were more and more dissatisfied with their deficient statesmanship, the responsible men over there believed that a successful war would be the most likely means of solving problems that otherwise would be beyond their power to solve.

Behind these men there stood the great international Jewish financial interests that control the banks and the Stock Exchange as well as the armament industry. And now, just as before, they scented the opportunity of doing their unsavory business. And so, just as before, there was no scruple about sacrificing the blood of the peoples. That was the beginning of this war. A few weeks later the State that was the third country in Europe, Poland, but had been reckless enough to allow herself to be used for the financial interests of these warmongers, was annihilated and destroyed.

In these circumstances I considered that I owed it to our German people and countless men and women in the opposite camps, who as individuals were as decent as they were innocent of blame, to make yet another appeal to the common sense and the conscience of these statesmen. On October 6, 1939, I therefore once more publicly stated that Germany had neither demanded nor intended to demand anything either from Britain or from France, that it was madness to continue the war and, above all, that the scourge of modern weapons of warfare, once they were brought into action, would inevitably ravage vast territories.

But just as the appeal I made on September 1, 1939, proved to be in vain, this renewed appeal met with indignant rejection. The British and their Jewish capitalist backers could find no other explanation for this appeal, which I had made on humanitarian grounds, than the assumption of weakness on the part of Germany.

They assured the people of Britain and France that Germany dreaded the clash to be expected in the spring of 1940 and was eager to make peace for fear of the annihilation that would then inevitably result.

Already at that time the Norwegian Government, misled by the stubborn insistence of Mr. Churchill's false prophecies, began to toy with the idea of a British landing on their soil, thereby contributing to the destruction of Germany by permitting their harbors and Swedish iron ore fields to be seized.

So sure were Mr. Churchill and Paul Reynaud of the success of their new scheme that finally, whether from sheer recklessness or perhaps under the influence of drink, they deemed it no longer necessary to make a secret of their intentions.

It was thanks to these two gentlemen's tendency to gossip that the German Government at that time gained cognizance of the plans being made against the Reich. A few weeks later this danger to Germany was eliminated. One of the boldest deeds of arms in the whole history of warfare frustrated the attack of the British and French armies against the right flank of our line of defense.

Immediately after the failure of these plans, increased pressure was exerted by the British warmongers upon Belgium and Holland. Now that the attack upon our sources for the supply of iron ore had proved unsuccessful, they aimed to advance the front to the Rhine by involving the Belgian and Dutch States and thus to threaten and paralyze our production centers for iron and steel.

On May 10 of last year perhaps the most memorable struggle in all German history commenced. The enemy front was broken up in a few days and the stage was then set for the operation that culminated in the greatest battle of annihilation in the history of the world. Thus France collapsed, Belgium and Holland were already occupied, and the battered remnants of the British expeditionary force were driven from the European continent, leaving their arms behind.

On July 19, 1940, I then convened the German Reichstag for the third time in order to render that great account which you all still remember. The meeting provided me with the opportunity of expressing the thanks of the nation to its soldiers in a form suited to the uniqueness of the event. Once again I seized the opportunity of urging the world to make peace. And what I foresaw and prophesied at that time happened. My offer of peace was misconstrued as a symptom of fear and cowardice.

The European and American warmongers succeeded once again in befogging the sound common sense of the masses, who can never hope to profit from this war, by conjuring up false pictures of new hope. Thus, finally, under pressure of public opinion, as formed by their press, they once more managed to induce the nation to continue this struggle.

Even my warnings against night bombings of the civilian population, as advocated by Mr. Churchill, were interpreted as a sign of German impotence. He, the most bloodthirsty or amateurish strategist that history has ever known, actually saw fit to believe that the reserve displayed for months by the German Air Force could be looked upon only as proof of their incapacity to fly by night.

So this man for months ordered his paid scribblers to deceive the British people into believing that the Royal Air Force alone - and no others - was in a position to wage war in this way, and that thus ways and means had been found to force the Reich to its knees by the ruthless onslaught of the British Air Force on the German civilian population in conjunction with the starvation blockade.

Again and again I uttered these warnings against this specific type of aerial warfare, and I did so for over three and a half months. That these warnings failed to impress Mr. Churchill does not surprise me in the least. For what does this man care for the lives of others? What does he care for culture or for architecture? When war broke out he stated clearly that he wanted to have his war, even though the cities of England might be reduced to ruins. So now he has got his war.

My assurances that from a given moment every one of his bombs would be returned if necessary a hundredfold failed to induce this man to consider even for an instant the criminal nature of his action. He professes not to be in the least depressed and he even assures us that the British people, too, after such bombing raids, greeted him with a joyous serenity, causing him to return to London refreshed by his visits to the stricken areas.

It is possible that this sight strengthened Mr. Churchill in his firm determination to continue the war in this way, and we are no less determined to continue to retaliate, if necessary, a hundred bombs for every one of his and to go on doing so until the British nation at last gets rid of this criminal and his methods.

The appeal to forsake me, made to the German nation by this fool and his satellites on May Day, of all days, are only to be explained either as symptomatic of a paralytic disease or of a drunkard's ravings. His abnormal state of mind also gave birth to a decision to transform the Balkans into a theater of war.

For over five years this man has been chasing around Europe like a madman in search of something that he could set on fire. Unfortunately, he again and again finds hirelings who open the gates of their country to this international incendiary.

After he had succeeded in the course of the past winter in persuading the British people by a wave of false assertions and pretensions that the German Reich, exhausted by the campaign in the preceding months, was completely spent, he saw himself obliged, in order to prevent an awakening of the truth, to create a fresh conflagration in Europe.

In so doing he returned to the project that had been in his mind as early as the autumn of 1939 and the spring of 1940. It was thought possible at the time to mobilize about 100 divisions in Britain's interest.

The sudden collapse which we witnessed in May and June of the past year forced these plans to be abandoned for the moment. But by the autumn of last year Mr. Churchill began to tackle this problem once again.

In the meantime, however, certain difficulties had arisen. As a result, Rumania, owing to internal changes, dropped out of England's political scheme.

In dealing with these conditions, I shall begin by giving you a brief outline of the aims of Germany's policy in the Balkans. As in the past, the Reich never pursued any territorial or any other selfish political interest in the Balkans. In other words, the Reich has never taken the slightest interest in territorial problems and internal conditions in these States for any selfish reason whatsoever.

On the other hand, the Reich has always endeavored to build up and to strengthen close economic ties with these States in particular. This, however, not only served the interests of the Reich but equally the interests of these countries themselves.

If any two national economic systems ever effectively complemented one another, that is especially the case regarding the Balkan States and Germany. Germany is an industrial country and requires foodstuffs and raw materials. The Balkan States are agrarian countries and are short of these raw materials. At the same time, they require industrial products.

It was therefore hardly surprising when Germany thus became the main business partner of the Balkan States. Nor was this in Germany's interest alone, but also in that of the Balkan peoples themselves.

AND NONE BUT OUR JEW-RIDDEN DEMOCRACIES, WHICH CAN THINK ONLY IN TERMS OF CAPITALISM, CAN MAINTAIN THAT IF ONE STATE DELIVERS MACHINERY TO ANOTHER STATE IT THEREBY DOMINATES THAT OTHER STATE. IN ACTUAL FACT SUCH DOMINATION, IF IT OCCURS, CAN BE ONLY A RECIPROCAL DOMINATION.

It is presumably easier to be without machinery than without food and raw materials. Consequently, the partner in need of raw material and foodstuffs would appear to be more tied down than the recipient of industrial products. IN THIS TRANSACTION THERE WAS NEITHER CONQUEROR NOR CONQUERED. THERE WERE ONLY PARTNERS.

The German Reich of the National Socialist revolution has prided itself on being a fair and decent partner, offering in exchange high-quality products instead of worthless democratic paper money. For these reasons the Reich was interested in only one thing if, indeed, there was any question of political interest, namely, in seeing that internally the business partner was firmly established on a sound and healthy basis.

THE APPLICATION OF THIS IDEA LED IN FACT NOT ONLY TO INCREASING PROSPERITY IN THESE COUNTRIES BUT ALSO TO THE BEGINNING OF MUTUAL CONFIDENCE. All the greater, however, became the endeavor of that world incendiary, Churchill, to put an end to this peaceful development and by shamelessly imposing upon these States utterly worthless British guarantees and promises of assistance to introduce into this peaceable European territory elements of unrest, uncertainty, distrust and, finally, conflict.

Originally, Rumania was first won over by these guarantees and later, of course, Greece. It has, meanwhile, probably been sufficiently demonstrated that he had absolutely no power of any kind to provide real help and that these guarantees were merely intended to rope these States in to follow the dangerous trend of filthy British politics.

RUMANIA HAS HAD TO PAY BITTERLY FOR THE GUARANTEES, WHICH WERE CALCULATED TO ESTRANGE HER FROM THE AXIS POWERS.

Greece, which least of all required such a guarantee, was offered her share to link her destiny to that of the country that provided her King with cash and orders.

EVEN TODAY I FEEL THAT I MUST, AS I BELIEVE IN THE INTEREST OF HISTORICAL ACCURACY, DISTINGUISH BETWEEN THE GREEK PEOPLE AND THAT THIN TOP LAYER OF CORRUPT LEADERS WHO, INSPIRED BY A KING WHO HAD NO EYES FOR THE DUTY OF TRUE LEADERSHIP, PREFERRED INSTEAD TO FURTHER THE AIMS OF BRITISH WAR POLITICS. To me this is a subject of profound regret.

Germany, with the faint hope of still being able to contribute in some way to a solution of the problem, had not severed relations with Greece. But even then I was bound in duty to point out before the whole world that we would not tacitly allow a revival of the old Salonika scheme of the Great War.

Unfortunately, my warning was not taken seriously enough. That we were determined, if the British tried to gain another foothold in Europe, to drive them back into the sea was not taken seriously enough.

The result was that the British began in an increasing degree to establish bases for the formation of a new Salonika army. They began by laying out airdromes and by establishing the necessary ground organization in the firm conviction that the occupation of the airdromes themselves could afterward be carried out very speedily.

Finally a continuous stream of transports brought equipment for an army which, according to Mr. Churchill's idea and plans, was to be landed in Greece. As I have said, already we were aware of this. For months we watched this entire strange procedure with attention, if with restraint.

The reverses suffered by the Italian Army in North Africa, owing to a certain material inferiority of their tanks and anti-tank guns, finally led Mr. Churchill to believe that the time was ripe to transfer the theater of war from Libya to Greece. He ordered the transport of the remaining tanks and of the infantry division, composed mainly of Anzacs, and was convinced that he could now complete his scheme, which was to set the Balkans aflame.

THUS DID MR. CHURCHILL COMMIT ONE OF THE GREATEST STRATEGIC BLUNDERS OF THIS WAR. As soon as there could be no further doubt regarding Britain's intentions of gaining a foothold in the Balkans, I took the necessary steps.

Germany, by keeping pace with these moves, assembled the

necessary forces for the purpose of counteracting any possible tricks of that gentleman. In this connection I must state categorically that this action was not directed against Greece.

The Duce did not even request me to place one single German division at his disposal for this purpose. He was convinced that with the advent of good weather his stand against Greece would have been brought to a successful conclusion. I was of the same opinion.

The concentration of German forces was therefore not made for the purpose of assisting the Italians against Greece. It was a precautionary measure against the British attempt under cover of the clamor caused by the Italo-Greek war to entrench themselves secretly in the Balkans in order to force the issue from that quarter on the model of the Salonika army during the World War, and, above all, to draw other elements into the whirlpool.

This hope was founded principally on two States, namely, Turkey and Yugoslavia. But with these very States I have striven during the years since I came into power to establish close co-operation.

The World War actually started from Belgrade. Nevertheless, the German people, who are by nature so ready to forgive and forget, felt no animosity toward that country. Turkey was our ally in the World War. The unfortunate outcome of that struggle weighed upon that country just as heavily as it did upon us.

The great genius who created the new Turkey was the first to set a wonderful example of recovery to our allies whom fortune had at that time deserted and whom fate had dealt so terrible a blow. Whereas Turkey, thanks to the practical attitude of her leaders, preserved her independence in carrying out her own resolutions, Yugoslavia fell a victim to British intrigue.

Most of you, especially my old Party comrades among you, know what efforts I have made to establish a straightforward understanding and indeed friendly relations between Germany and Yugoslavia. In pursuance of this aim Herr von Ribbentrop, our Minister of Foreign Affairs, submitted to the Yugoslav Government proposals that were so outstanding and so fair that at least even the Yugoslav State of that time seemed to become increasingly eager for such close co-operation.

Germany had no intention of starting a war in the Balkans. On the contrary, it was our honest intention as far as possible to contribute to a settlement of the conflict with Greece by means that would be tolerable to the legitimate wishes of Italy.

The Duce not only consented to but lent his full support to our efforts to bring Yugoslavia into a close community of interests with our peace aims. Thus it finally became possible to induce the Yugoslav Government to join the Threepower Pact, which made no demands whatever on Yugoslavia but only offered that country advantages.

Thus on March 26 of this year a pact was signed in Vienna that offered the Yugoslav State the greatest future conceivable and could have assured peace for the Balkans. Believe me, gentlemen, on that day I left the beautiful city of the Danube truly happy not only because it seemed as though almost eight years of foreign policies had received their reward but also because I believed that perhaps at the last moment German intervention in the Balkans might not be necessary.

We were all stunned by the news of that coup, carried through by a handful of bribed conspirators who had brought about the event that caused the British Prime Minister to declare in joyous words that at last he had something good to report.

YOU WILL SURELY UNDERSTAND, GENTLEMEN, THAT WHEN I HEARD THIS I AT ONCE GAVE ORDERS TO ATTACK YUGOSLAVIA. To treat the, German Reich in this way is impossible. One cannot spent years in concluding a treaty that is in the interest of the other party merely to discover that this treaty has not only been broken overnight but also that it has been answered by the insulting of the representative of the German Reich, by the threatening of his military attache, 'by the injuring of the aide de camp of this attache', by the maltreating of numerous other Germans, by demolishing property, by laying waste the homes of German citizens and by terrorizing.

GOD KNOWS THAT I WANTED PEACE. But I can do nothing but protect the interests of the Reich with those means which, thank God, are at our disposal. I made my decision at that moment all the more calmly because I knew that I was in accord with Bulgaria, who had always remained unshaken in her loyalty to the German Reich, and with the equally justified indignation of Hungary.

Both of our old allies in the World War were bound to regard this action as a provocation emanating from the State that once before had set the whole of Europe on fire and had been guilty of the indescribable sufferings that befell Germany, Hungary, and Bulgaria in consequence.

The general directions of operations issued by me through the Supreme Command of the German forces on March 27 confronted the Army and the Air Force with a formidable task. By a mere turn of the hand an additional campaign had to be prepared. Units that had already arrived had to be moved about. Supplies of armaments had to be assured and the air force had to take over numerous improvised airports, parts of which were still under water.

WITHOUT THE SYMPATHETIC ASSISTANCE OF HUNGARY AND THE EXTREMELY LOYAL ATTITUDE OF RUMANIA IT WOULD HAVE BEEN VERY DIFFICULT TO CARRY OUT MY ORDERS IN THE SHORT TIME ENVISAGED.

I fixed April 6 as the day on which the attack was to begin. The main plan of operation was: First, to proceed with an army coming from Bulgaria against Thrace in Greece in the direction of the Aegean Sea.

The main striking strength of this army lay in its right wing; which was to force a passage through to Salonika by using mountain divisions and a division of tanks; second, to thrust forward with a second army with the object of establishing connection as speedily as possible with the Italian forces advancing from Albania. These two operations were to begin on April 6.

Third, a further operation, beginning on the eighth, provided for the break-through of an army from Bulgaria with the object of reaching the neighborhood of Belgrade. In conjunction with this, a German army corps was to occupy the Banat on the tenth.

In connection with these operations general agreement had been made with our allies, Italy and Hungary. Agreements as to co-operation had also been reached between the two air forces. The command of the German Armies operating against Macedonia and Greece was placed in the hands of Field Marshal von List, who had already particularly distinguished himself in the previous campaigns. Once more and under the most exacting conditions he carried out the task confronting him in truly superior fashion.

The forces advancing against Yugoslavia from the southwest and from Hungary were commanded by Col. Gen. von Weick. He, too, in a very short time with the forces under his command reached his objective.

The Army and SS detachments operating under Field Marshal von Brauchitsch, as Commander in Chief, and the Chief of the General Staff, Col. Gen. Halder, forced the Greek Army in Thrace to capitulate after only five days, established contact with the Italian forces advancing from Albania, occupied Salonika, and thus generally prepared the way for the difficult and glorious break-through via Larissa to Athens.

These operations were crowned by the occupation of the Peloponnesus and numerous Greek islands. A detailed appreciation of the achievements will be given by the German High Command.

The Air Force under the personal command of Reich Marshal Goering was divided into two main groups, commanded by Col. Gen. Loehr and General von Richthofen. It was their task, first, to shatter the enemy air force and to smash its ground organization; second, to attack every important military objective in the conspirators' headquarters at Belgrade, thus eliminating it from the very outset; third, by every manner of active co-operation everywhere with the fighting German troops to break the enemy's resistance, to impede the enemy's flight, to prevent as far as possible his embarkation.

The German armed forces have truly surpassed themselves in this campaign. There is only one way of characterizing that campaign:

Nothing is impossible for the German soldier. Historical justice, however, obliges me to say that of the opponents that have taken up arms against us, MOST PARTICULARLY THE GREEK SOLDIERS, HAVE FOUGHT WITH THE GREATEST BRAVERY AND CONTEMPT OF DEATH. They only capitulated when further resistance became impossible and therefore useless.

But I am now compelled to speak of the enemy who is the main cause of this conflict. As a German and as a soldier I consider it unworthy ever to revile a fallen enemy. But it seems to me to be necessary to defend the truth from the wild exaggerations of a man who as a soldier is a bad politician and as a politician is an equally bad soldier.

Mr. Churchill, who started this struggle, is endeavoring, as with regard to Norway or Dunkerque, to say something that sooner or later might perhaps he twisted around to resemble success. I do not consider that honorable but in his case it is understandable.

The gift Mr. Churchill possesses is the gift to lie with a pious expression on his face and to distort the truth until finally glorious victories are made out of the most terrible defeats.

A British Army of 60,000 to 70,000 men landed in Greece. Before the catastrophe the same man maintained, moreover, that it consisted of 240,000 men. The object of this army was to attack Germany from the south, inflict a defeat upon her, and from this point as in 1918 turn the tide of the war.

I prophesied more correctly than Mr. Churchill in my last speech, in which I announced that wherever the British might set foot on the Continent they would be attacked by us and driven into the sea.

Now, with his brazen effrontery, he asserts that this war has cost us 75,000 lives. He causes his presumably not over-intelligent fellow-countrymen to be informed by one of his paid creatures that the British, after having slain enormous masses of Germans, finally turned away from sheer abhorrence of the slaughter and, strictly speaking, withdrew for this reason alone.

I will now present to you the results of this campaign in a few short figures. In the course of the operations against Yugoslavia there were the following numbers of purely Serbian prisoners, leaving out soldiers of German origin and some other groups, 6,198 officers, 313,864 men.

The number of Greek prisoners, 8,000 officers and 210,000 men, has not the same significance. The number of Englishmen, New Zealanders and Australians taken prisoner exceeds 9,000 officers and men.

The German share of the booty alone, according to the estimates at present available, amounts to more than half a million rifles, far more than 1,000 guns, many thousand machine-guns and anti-aircraft machine-guns, vehicles, and large amounts of ammunition . . . .

The losses of the German Army and the German Air Force as well as those of the SS troops in this campaign are the smallest that we have ever suffered so far. The German armed forces have in fighting against Yugoslavia and Greece as well as against the British in Greece lost:

Army and SS Troops - Fifty-seven officers and 1,042 non-commissioned officers and men killed, 181 officers and 3,571 non-commissioned officers and men wounded, and 13 officers and 372 non-commissioned officers and men missing.

Air Force - Ten officers and 42 non-commissioned officers and men killed and 36 officers and 104 non-commissioned officers and men missing.

Once more I can only repeat that we feel the hardship of the sacrifice borne by the families concerned. The entire German nation expresses to them its heartfelt gratitude.

Taking the measures as a whole, however, the losses suffered are so small that they constitute supreme justification, first, for the planning and timing of this campaign; second for the conduct of operations; third, for the manner in which they were carried through.

The training of our officers is excellent beyond comparison The high standard of efficiency of our soldiers, the superiority of our equipment, the quality of our munitions and the indomitable courage of all ranks have combined to lead at such small sacrifice to a success of truly decisive historical importance.

Churchill, one of the most hopeless dabblers in strategy, thus managed to lose two theaters of war at one single blow. The fact that this man, who in any other country would be court-martialed, gained fresh admiration as Prime Minister cannot be construed as an expression of magnanimity such as was accorded by Roman senators to generals honorably defeated in battle. It is merely proof of that perpetual blindness with which the gods afflict those whom they are about to destroy.

The consequences of this campaign are extraordinary. In view of the fact that a small set of conspirators in Belgrade again were able to foment trouble in the service of extracontinental interests, the radical elimination of this danger means the removal of an element of tension for the whole of Europe.

The Danube as an important waterway is thus safeguarded against any further act of sabotage. Traffic has been resumed in full.

Apart from the modest correction of its frontiers, which were infringed as a result of the outcome of the World War, the Reich has no special territorial interests in these parts. As far as politics are concerned we are merely interested in safeguarding peace in this region, while in the realm of economics we wish to see an order that will allow the production of goods to be developed and the exchange of products to be resumed in the interests of all.

It is, however, only in accordance with supreme justice if those interests are also taken into account that are founded upon ethnographical, historical, or economic conditions.

I can assure you that I look into the future with perfect tranquility and great confidence. The German Reich and its allies represent power, military, economic and, above all, in moral respects, which is superior to any possible coalition in the world. The German armed forces will always do their part whenever it may be necessary. The confidence of the German people will always accompany their soldiers.

■

Biographical Sketch: Diana, Princess of Wales (July 1, 1961–August 31, 1997) was the first wife of Charles, Prince of Wales, eldest son and heir apparent of Elizabeth II. Her romance with the Prince of Wales began in 1980 and they got married on July 29, 1981 at St Paul's Cathedral. Diana was the first English woman to marry an heir to the throne in over 300 years. However, the marriage was a sour affair and Diana often attempted suicide. Despite her problems, she was a devoted mother to her two sons, Prince William and Prince Harry. She worked tirelessly for charity, and was loved by the public for her warmth and humanity.

Speech By: Diana, Princess of Wales

Topic: Women and Children with AIDS

Date: September 8, 1993 in Edinburgh

Some sections of the media would have us believe that the dark shadow of AIDS is fading away. The predicted explosion has failed to happen and retreated back to those who've so often been condemned or ignored.

Yet common sense and the testimonies of healthcare workers, worldwide, tell us a very different story. The truth is that most people infected by HIV are heterosexual and the disease is spreading, throughout the world, at a staggering rate.

By the year two thousand–only seven years from now–even the most conservative estimates predict there will be more than thirty million people, worldwide, with HIV–equivalent to more than half the population of the United Kingdom!

Mothers and chi dren are being 'infected' or 'affected' by the Aids virus in greater and greater numbers, every single day.

A mother with HIV or Aids doesn't give up the responsibility of caring for her children easily. Often she is the sole parent, the wage earner, the provider of food, the organiser of daily life, the nurse to other sick members of the family, including her own children. Relentless demands continue to be placed on her, at a time when her own health and strength are falling away.

As well as the physical drain on her energy, a mother with HIV carries the grief and guilt that she probably won't see her healthy children through to independence. If she has passed on HIV to one of her children, she will have to witness their illness while trying to make something of their short life. Worrying as to what will happen to them if she dies first.

Trying to plan for her surviving children's futures won't be an easy task! At what stage should she give up her role as a parent? Who can she rely on to take care of them? Where can she find the right kind of support to decide what is best for them? How can she be sure that her family history and traditions won't be lost?

Yet the biggest fear of the mothers I've met with HIV or AIDS is not their disease. They've learnt to live with their disease, especially, as for much of the time they are feeling well! No, what terrifies them most, is other people! For despite information about Aids being available now for nearly ten years, these women still face harassment, job loss, isolation, even physical aggression, if their family secret gets out.

How then is it possible for them to decide the moment to explain to their children what is happening in their lives? Do they tell the neighbours? Do they tell their children's school? Is there anyone they can truly trust or is it safer and wiser to struggle on alone?

Yet these mothers don't ask for sympathy. Their need is for understanding. To be allowed to live a full and active life. To be given the support to love and care for their children, for as long as they can, without carrying the added burden of our ignorance and fear.

And what of the children who live with HIV every day? Not because they're necessarily ill themselves, but because their family life includes a mother, father, brother or sister who has the virus. How will we help them come to terms with the loss of the people they love? How will we help them to grieve? How will we help them to feel secure about their future?

These children need to feel the same things as other children. To play, to laugh and cry, to make friends, to enjoy the ordinary experiences of childhood. To feel loved and nurtured and included by the world they live in, without the stigma that AIDS continues to attract.

By listening to their needs, really listening, perhaps we can find the best way of helping these children to face their future with greater confidence and hope.

The effect HIV and AIDS has on mothers and children, when the disease is allowed to spread unchecked, was brought home to me on my recent visit to Zimbabwe. I saw for myself the very personal tragedies whole families were suffering.

The damage it was doing to their communities, to the country as a whole, both socially and economically, was devastating.

Yet the support these families were given by those around them was a lesson for us all. They were being treated with compassion and respect, by their friends and neighbours, for what they were having to go through. And were still accepted as an important part of their community, not as outcasts to be ignored.

Here in the United Kingdom the number of women and children known to be infected or affected by HIV or AIDS is still comparatively small. But if we continue to believe that AIDS is someone else's problem, we too, could so easily be facing the same devastating destruction of our nation's way of life that is already happening in other parts of the world.

In my daily life I've seen for myself the tremendous work being done by the many charities and government organisations who are searching for new ways of tackling the dilemma of AIDS. The importance of this conference, here in Edinburgh, cannot be underestimated. It brings together those people who represent milestones of achievement around the world in dealing with the complexities of HIV and AIDS in mothers and children. And also, those who've pushed back the boundaries of our understanding of how the infection is transmitted and how it can be treated. Your exchange of ideas and experiences will, I am sure, make a difference to the future well-being of us all.

I feel certain, we as a nation still need to develop a deeper understanding of what AIDS really is. To possibly, be just a little more aware and just a little less embarrassed about how the virus is transmitted, even when we don't really see ourselves at risk. In that way, perhaps, we may play a small part in helping to protect a person we love from becoming infected with HIV.

For those mothers and children already living under the dark shadow of AIDS we need to help them back into the light. To reassure them. To respect and support their needs. And maybe, we will learn from them, how to live our own life more fully, for however long it is.

■

Biographical Sketch: Avul Pakir Jainulabdeen Abdul Kalam Maraikkayar (born October 15, 1931) is usually referred to as Dr. A.P.J. Abdul Kalam. He is the current President of India. Born in Tamil Nadu, he is a notable scientist and engineer, and is often referred to as the 'Missile Man of India' for his work. He is considered a leading, progressive, mentor, innovator and visionary. He has received honorary doctorates from at least thirty universities. He has also received India's three highest civilian honours: the Padma Bhushan in 1981; the Padma Vibhushan in 1990; and the Bharat Ratna in 1997.

Speech By: Dr. APJ Abdul Kalam

Topic: Three Visions

I have three visions for India.

In 3,000 years of our history people from all over the world have come and invaded us, captured our lands, conquered our minds. From Alexander onwards. The Greeks, the Turks, the Moguls, the Portuguese, the British, the French, the Dutch, all of them came and looted us, took over what was ours. Yet we have not done this to any other nation. We have not conquered anyone. We have not grabbed their land, their culture, their history and tried to enforce our way of life on them. Why? Because we respect the freedom of others. That is why my first vision is that of FREEDOM. I believe that India got its first vision of this in 1857, when we started the war of independence. It is this freedom that we must protect and nurture and build on. If we are not free, no one will respect us.

My second vision for India is DEVELOPMENT. For fifty years we have been a developing nation. It is time we see ourselves as a developed nation. We are among top 5 nations of the world in terms of GDP. We have 10 per cent growth rate in most areas. Our poverty levels are falling. Our achievements are being globally recognized today. Yet we lack the self-confidence to see ourselves as a developed nation, self-reliant and self-assured. Isn't this incorrect?

I have a THIRD vision. India must stand up to the world. Because I believe that unless India stands up to the world, no one will respect us. Only strength respects strength. We must be strong not only as a military power but also as an economic power. Both must go hand-in-hand. My good fortune was to have worked with three great minds. Dr. Vikram Sarabhai of the Department of space, Professor Satish Dhawan, who succeeded him and Dr. Brahm Prakash, father of nuclear material. I was lucky to have worked with all three of them closely and consider this the great opportunity of my life.

I see four milestones in my career:

ONE: Twenty years I spent in ISRO. I was given the opportunity to be the project director for India's first satellite launch vehicle, SLV3. The one that launched Rohini. These years played a very important role in my life of Scientist.

TWO: After my ISRO years, I joined DRDO and got a chance to be the part of India's missile programme. It was my second bliss when Agni met its mission requirements in 1994.

THREE: The Department. of Atomic Energy and DRDO had this tremendous partnership in the recent nuclear tests, on May 11 and 13. This was the third bliss. The joy of participating with my team in these nuclear tests and proving to the world that India can make it, that we are no longer a developing nation but one of them. It made me feel very proud as an Indian. The fact that we have now developed for Agni a re-entry structure, for which we have developed this new material. A Very light material called carbon-carbon.

FOUR: One day an orthopedic surgeon from Nizam Institute of Medical Sciences visited my laboratory. He lifted the material and found it so light that he took me to his hospital and showed me his patients. There were these little girls and boys with heavy metallic calipers weighing over three kg. each, dragging their feet around. He said to me: Please remove the pain of my patients. In three weeks, we made these Floor reaction Orthosis 300 gram calipers and took them to the orthopedic centre. The children didn't believe their eyes. From dragging around a three kg. load on their legs, they could now move around! Their parents had tears in their eyes. That was my fourth bliss!

Why is the media here so negative? Why are we in India so embarrassed to recognize our own strengths, our achievements? We are such a great nation. We have so many amazing success stories but we refuse to acknowledge them. Why? We are the first in milk production. We are number one in Remote sensing satellites. We are the second largest producer of wheat. We are the second largest producer of rice. Look at Dr. Sudarshan, he has transferred the tribal village into a self-sustaining, self-driving unit. There are millions of such achievements but our media is only obsessed in the bad news and failures and disasters.

I was in Tel Aviv once and I was reading the Israeli newspaper. It was the day after a lot of attacks and bombardments and deaths had taken place. The Hamas had struck. But the front page of the newspaper had the picture of a Jewish gentleman who in five years had transformed his desert land into an orchid and a granary. It was this inspiring picture that everyone woke up to. The gory details of killings, bombardments, deaths, were inside in the newspaper, buried among other news. In India we only read about death, sickness, terrorism, crime. Why are we so

NEGATIVE? Another question: Why are we, as a nation so obsessed with foreign things? We want foreign TVs, we want foreign shirts. We want foreign technology. Why this obsession with everything imported. Do we not realize that self-respect comes with self-reliance?

I was in Hyderabad giving this lecture, when a 14 year old girl asked me for my autograph. I asked her what her goal in life is: She replied: I want to live in a developed India. For her, you and I will have to build this developed India. You must proclaim. India is not an under-developed nation; it is a highly developed nation.

Allow me to come back with vengeance. Got 10 minutes for your country?

YOU say that our government is inefficient. YOU say that our laws are too old. YOU say that the municipality does not pick up the garbage. YOU say that the phones don't work, the railways are a joke, the airline is the worst in the world, mails never reach their destination. YOU say that our country has been fed to the dogs and is the absolute pits. YOU say, say and say.

What do YOU do about it? Take a person on his way to Singapore. Give him a name - YOURS. Give him a face - YOURS. YOU walk out of the airport and you are at your International best. In Singapore you don't throw cigarette butts on the roads or eat in the stores. YOU are as proud of their Underground Links as they are. You pay $5 (approx. Rs. 60) to drive through Orchard Road (equivalent of Mahim Causeway or Pedder Road) between 5 PM and 8 PM.

YOU comeback to the parking lot to punch your parking ticket if you have over stayed in a restaurant or a shopping mall irrespective of your status identity. In Singapore you don't say anything, DO YOU? YOU wouldn't dare to eat in public during Ramadan, in Dubai. YOU would not dare to go out without your head covered in Jeddah. YOU would not dare to buy an employee of the telephone exchange in London at 10 pounds (Rs. 650) a month to, "see to it that my STD and ISD calls are billed to someone else." YOU would not dare to speed beyond 55 mph (88 kph) in Washington and then tell the traffic cop, "Jaanta hai sala main kaun hoon (Do you know who I am?)? I am so and so's son. Take your two bucks and get lost." YOU wouldn't chuck an empty coconut shell anywhere other than the garbage pail on the beaches in Australia and New Zealand. Why don't YOU spit Paan on the streets of Tokyo? Why don't YOU use examination jockeys or buy fake certificates in Boston? We are still talking of the same YOU. YOU who can respect and conform to a foreign system in other countries but cannot in your own. You who will throw papers and cigarettes on the road the moment you touch Indian ground. If you can be an involved and appreciative citizen in an alien country why cannot you be the same here in India. Once in an interview, the famous Ex-municipal commissioner of Bombay Mr.Tinaikar had a point to make. "Rich people's dogs are walked on the streets to leave their affluent droppings all over the place," he said. "And then the same people turn around to criticize and blame the authorities for inefficiency and dirty pavements. What do they expect the officers to do? Go down with a broom every time their dog feels the pressure in his bowels? In America every dog owner has to clean up after his pet has done the job. Same in Japan. Will the Indian citizen do that here?" He's right. We go to the polls to choose a government and after that forfeit all responsibility. We sit back wanting to be pampered and expect the government to do everything for us whilst our contribution is totally negative. We expect the government to clean up but we are not going to stop chucking garbage all over the place nor are we going to stop to pick up a stray piece of paper and throw it in the bin. We expect the railways to provide clean bathrooms but we are not going to learn the proper use of bathrooms. We want Indian Airlines and Air India to provide the best of food and toiletries but we are not going to stop pilfering at the least opportunity.

This applies even to the staff who is known not to pass on the service to the public. When it comes to burning social issues like those related to women, dowry, girl child and others, we make loud drawing room protestations and continue to do the reverse at home. Our excuse? "It's the whole system which has to change, how will it matter if I alone forego my sons' rights to a dowry." So who's going to change the system? What does a system consist of? Very conveniently for us it consists of our neighbours, other households, other cities, other communities and the government. But definitely not me and YOU. When it comes to us actually making a positive contribution to the system we lock ourselves along with our families into a safe cocoon and look into the distance at countries far away and wait for a Mr. Clean to come along and work miracles for us with a majestic sweep of his hand. Or we leave the country and run away. Like lazy cowards hounded by our fears we run to America to bask in their glory and praise their system. When New York becomes insecure we run to England. When England experiences unemployment, we take the next flight out to the Gulf. When the Gulf is war struck, we demand to be rescued and brought home by the Indian government. Everybody is out to abuse and rape the country. Nobody thinks of feeding the system. Our conscience is mortgaged to money.

Dear Indians, the article is highly thought inductive, calls for a great deal of introspection and pricks one's conscience too....I am echoing J. F. Kennedy's words to his fellow Americans to relate to Indians.....

"ASK WHAT WE CAN DO FOR INDIA AND DO WHAT HAS TO BE DONE TO MAKE INDIA WHAT AMERICA AND OTHER WESTERN COUNTRIES ARE TODAY."

Let's do what India needs from us.

■

Biographical Sketch: Charles Edward Maurice Spencer, 9th Earl Spencer (born May 20, 1964) is the second and only surviving son of the 8th Earl Spencer by his first wife, the former Frances Burke Roche. The youngest of his three elder sisters was Diana, Princess of Wales.

Speech By: Earl Charles Spencer

Topic: Funeral Speech (Eulogy) following the death of Diana, Princess of Wales

Date: September 6, 1997

I stand before you today the representative of a family in grief, in a country in mourning before a world in shock. We are all united not only in our desire to pay our respects to Diana but rather in our need to do so. For such was her extraordinary appeal that the tens of millions of people taking part in this service all over the world via television and radio who never actually met her, feel that they too lost someone close to them in the early hours of Sunday morning. It is a more remarkable tribute to Diana than I can ever hope to offer her today.

"No Need for Royal Title"

Diana was the very essence of compassion, of duty, of style, of beauty. All over the world she was a symbol of selfless humanity. All over the world, a standard bearer for the rights of the truly downtrodden, a very British girl who transcended nationality. Someone with a natural nobility who was classless and who proved in the last year that she needed no royal title to continue to generate her particular brand of magic.

Today is our chance to say thank you for the way you brightened our lives, even though God granted you but half a life. We will all feel cheated always that you were taken from us so young and yet we must learn to be grateful that you came along at all. Only now that you are gone do we truly appreciate what we are now without and we want you to know that life without you is very, very difficult.

We have all despaired at our loss over the past week and only the strength of the message you gave us through your years of giving has afforded us the strength to move forward.

"Great Gift of Intuition"

There is a temptation to rush to canonise your memory, there is no need to do so. You stand tall enough as a human being of unique qualities not to need to be seen as a saint. Indeed to sanctify your memory would be to miss out on the very core of your being, your wonderfully mischievous sense of humour with a laugh that bent you double.

Your joy for life transmitted where ever you took your smile and the sparkle in those unforgettable eyes. Your boundless energy which you could barely contain.

But your greatest gift was your intuition and it was a gift you used wisely. This is what underpinned all your other wonderful attributes and if we look to analyse what it was about you that had such a wide appeal we find it in your instinctive feel for what was really important in all our lives.

Without your God-given sensitivity we would be immersed in greater ignorance at the anguish of Aids and HIV sufferers, the plight of the homeless, the isolation of lepers, the random destruction of landmines.

"Innermost Feelings of Suffering"

Diana explained to me once that it was her innermost feelings of suffering that made it possible for her to connect with her constituency of the rejected.

And here we come to another truth about her. For all the status, the glamour, the applause, Diana remained throughout a very insecure person at heart, almost childlike in her desire to do good for others so she could release herself from deep feelings of unworthiness of which her eating disorders were merely a symptom.

The world sensed this part of her character and cherished her for her vulnerability whilst admiring her for her honesty.

The last time I saw Diana was on July 1, her birthday in London, when typically she was not taking time to celebrate her special day with friends but was guest of honour at a special charity fundraising evening. She sparkled of course, but I would rather cherish the days I spent with her in March when she came to visit me and my children in our home in South Africa. I am proud of the fact apart from when she was on display meeting President Mandela we managed to contrive to stop the ever-present paparazzi from getting a single picture of her - that meant a lot to her.

These were days I will always treasure. It was as if we had been transported back to our childhood when we spent such an enormous amount of time together - the two youngest in the family.

Fundamentally she had not changed at all from the big sister who mothered me as a baby, fought with me at school and endured those long train journeys between our parents' homes with me at weekends.

It is a tribute to her level-headedness and strength that despite the most bizarre-like life imaginable after her childhood, she remained intact, true to herself.

"Diana's Goodness Threatened the Media"

There is no doubt that she was looking for a new direction in her life at this time. She talked endlessly of getting away from England, mainly because of the treatment that she received at the hands of the newspapers. I don't think she ever understood why her genuinely good intentions were sneered at by the media, why there appeared to be a permanent quest on their behalf to bring her down. It is baffling.

My own and only explanation is that genuine goodness is threatening to those at the opposite end of the moral spectrum. It is a point to remember that of all the ironies about Diana, perhaps the greatest was this–a girl given the name of the ancient goddess of hunting was, in the end, the most hunted person of the modern age.

She would want us today to pledge ourselves to protecting her beloved boys William and Harry from a similar fate and I do this here Diana on your behalf. We will not allow them to suffer the anguish that used regularly to drive you to tearful despair.

"Blood Family Will Protect Sons"

And beyond that, on behalf of your mother and sisters, I pledge that we, your blood family, will do all we can to continue the imaginative way in which you were steering these two exceptional young men so that their souls are not simply immersed by duty and tradition but can sing openly as you planned.

We fully respect the heritage into which they have both been born and will always respect and encourage them in their royal role but we, like you, recognise the need for them to experience as many different aspects of life as possible to arm them spiritually and emotionally for the years ahead. I know you would have expected nothing less from us.

William and Harry, we all cared desperately for you today. We are all chewed up with the sadness at the loss of a woman who was not even our mother. How great your suffering is, we cannot even imagine.

I would like to end by thanking God for the small mercies he has shown us at this dreadful time. For taking Diana at her most beautiful and radiant and when she had joy in her private life. Above all we give thanks for the life of a woman I am so proud to be able to call my sister, the unique, the complex, the extraordinary and irreplaceable Diana whose beauty, both internal and external, will never be extinguished from our minds.

■

Biographical Sketch: Franklin Delano Roosevelt (January 30, 1882–April 12, 1945) was the 32nd President of the United States. Ranked as one of the three greatest U.S. presidents in scholarly surveys, he was a central figure of the 20th century.

During the Great Depression of the 1930s, Roosevelt created the New Deal to provide relief for the unemployed, recovery of the economy, and reform of the economic system.

Speech By: Franklin Delano Roosevelt

Topic: The Four Freedoms

Date: January 6, 1941

Mr. President, Mr. Speaker, members of the 77th Congress:

I address you, the members of this new Congress, at a moment unprecedented in the history of the union. I use the word "unprecedented" because at no previous time has American security been as seriously threatened from without as it is today.

Since the permanent formation of our government under the Constitution in 1789, most of the periods of crisis in our history have related to our domestic affairs. And, fortunately, only one of these–the four-year war between the States–ever threatened our national unity. Today, thank God, 130,000,000 Americans in 48 States have forgotten points of the compass in our national unity.

It is true that prior to 1914 the United States often has been disturbed by events in other continents. We have even engaged in two wars with European nations and in a number of undeclared wars in the West Indies, in the Mediterranean and in the Pacific, for the maintenance of American rights and for the principles of peaceful commerce. But in no case had a serious threat been raised against our national safety or our continued independence.

What I seek to convey is the historic truth that the United States as a nation has at all times maintained opposition–clear, definite opposition–to any attempt to lock us in behind an ancient Chinese wall while the procession of civilization went past. Today, thinking of our children and of their children, we oppose enforced isolation for ourselves or for any other part of the Americas.

That determination of ours, extending over all these years, was proved, for example, in the early days during the quarter century of wars following the French Revolution. While the Napoleonic struggles did threaten interests of the United States because of the French foothold in the West Indies and in Louisiana, and while we engaged in the War of 1812 to vindicate our right to peaceful trade, it is nevertheless clear that neither France nor Great Britain nor any other nation was aiming at domination of the whole world.

And in like fashion, from 1815 to 1914–ninety-nine years–no single war in Europe or in Asia constituted a real threat against our future or against the future of any other American nation.

Except in the Maximilian interlude in Mexico, no foreign power sought to establish itself in this hemisphere. And the strength of the British fleet in the Atlantic has been a friendly strength; it is still a friendly strength.

Even when the World War broke out in 1914, it seemed to contain only small threat of danger to our own American future. But as time went on, as we remember, the American people began to visualize what the downfall of democratic nations might mean to our own democracy.

We need not overemphasize imperfections in the peace of Versailles. We need not harp on failure of the democracies to deal with problems of world reconstruction. We should remember that the peace of 1919 was far less unjust than the kind of pacification which began even before Munich, and which is being carried on under the new order of tyranny that seeks to spread over every continent today. The American people have unalterably set their faces against that tyranny.

I suppose that every realist knows that the democratic way of life is at this moment being directly assailed in every part of the world–assailed either by arms or by secret spreading of poisonous propaganda by those who seek to destroy unity and promote discord in nations that are still at peace. During 16 long months this assault has blotted out the whole pattern of democratic life in an appalling number of independent nations, great and small. And the assailants are still on the march, threatening other nations, great and small.

Therefore, as your President, performing my constitutional duty to "give to the Congress information of the state of the union," I find it unhappily necessary to report that the future and the safety of our country and of our democracy are overwhelmingly involved in events far beyond our borders.

Armed defense of democratic existence is now being gallantly waged in four continents. If that defense fails, all the population and all the resources of Europe and Asia, and Africa and Austral-Asia will be dominated by conquerors. And let us remember that the total of those populations in those four continents, the total of those populations and their resources greatly exceed the sum total of the population and the resources of the whole of the Western Hemisphere–yes, many times over.

In times like these it is immature–and, incidentally, untrue–for anybody to brag that an unprepared America, single-handed and with one hand tied behind its back, can hold off the whole world.

No realistic American can expect from a dictator's peace international generosity, or return of true independence, or world disarmament, or freedom of expression, or freedom of religion–or even good business. Such a peace would bring no security for us or for our neighbors. Those who would give up essential liberty to purchase a little temporary safety deserve neither liberty nor safety.

As a nation we may take pride in the fact that we are soft-hearted; but we cannot afford to be soft-headed. We must always be wary of those who with sounding brass and a tinkling cymbal preach the "ism" of appeasement. We must especially beware of that small group of selfish men who would clip the wings of the American eagle in order to feather their own nests.

I have recently pointed out how quickly the tempo of modern warfare could bring into our very midst the physical attack which we must eventually expect if the dictator nations win this war.

There is much loose talk of our immunity from immediate and direct invasion from across the seas. Obviously, as long as the British Navy retains its power, no such danger exists. Even if there were no British Navy, it is not probable that any enemy would be stupid enough to attack us by landing troops in the United States from across thousands of miles of ocean, until it had acquired strategic bases from which to operate.

But we learn much from the lessons of the past years in Europe–particularly the lesson of Norway, whose essential seaports were captured by treachery and surprise built up over a series of years. The first phase of the invasion of this hemisphere would not be the landing of regular troops. The necessary strategic points would be occupied by secret agents and by their dupes–and great numbers of them are already here and in Latin America. As long as the aggressor nations maintain the offensive they, not we, will choose the time and the place and the method of their attack.

And that is why the future of all the American Republics is today in serious danger. That is why this annual message to the Congress is unique in our history. That is why every member of the executive branch of the government and every member of the Congress face great responsibility, great accountability. The need of the moment is that our actions and our policy should be devoted primarily–almost exclusively–to meeting this foreign peril. For all our domestic problems are now a part of the great emergency.

Just as our national policy in internal affairs has been based upon a decent respect for the rights and the dignity of all our fellow men within our gates, so our national policy in foreign affairs has been based on a decent respect for the rights and the dignity of all nations, large and small. And the justice of morality must and will win in the end.

Our national policy is this:

First, by an impressive expression of the public will and without regard to partisanship, we are committed to all-inclusive national defense.

Secondly, by an impressive expression of the public will and without regard to partisanship, we are committed to full support of all those resolute people everywhere who are resisting aggression and are thereby keeping war away from our hemisphere. By this support we express our determination that the democratic cause shall prevail, and we strengthen the defense and the security of our own nation.

Third, by an impressive expression of the public will and without regard to partisanship, we are committed to the proposition that principles of morality and considerations for our own security will never permit us to acquiesce in a peace dictated by aggressors and sponsored by appeasers. We know that enduring peace cannot be bought at the cost of other people's freedom.

In the recent national election there was no substantial difference between the two great parties in respect to that national policy. No issue was fought out on this line before the American electorate. And today it is abundantly evident that American citizens everywhere are demanding and supporting speedy and complete action in recognition of obvious danger.

Therefore, the immediate need is a swift and driving increase in our armament production. Leaders of industry and labor have responded to our summons. Goals of speed have been set. In some cases these goals are being reached ahead of time. In some cases we are on schedule; in other cases there are slight but not serious delays. And in some cases–and, I am sorry to say, very important cases–we are all concerned by the slowness of the accomplishment of our plans.

The Army and Navy, however, have made substantial progress during the past year. Actual experience is improving and speeding up our methods of production with every passing day. And today's best is not good enough for tomorrow.

I am not satisfied with the progress thus far made. The men in charge of the program represent the best in training, in ability, and in patriotism. They are not satisfied with the progress thus far made. None of us will be satisfied until the job is done.

No matter whether the original goal was set too high or too low, our objective is quicker and better results.

To give you two illustrations:

We are behind schedule in turning out finished airplanes. We are working day and night to solve the innumerable problems and to catch up.

We are ahead of schedule in building warships, but we are working to get even further ahead of that schedule.

To change a whole nation from a basis of peacetime production of implements of peace to a basis of wartime production of implements of war is no small task. And the greatest difficulty comes at the beginning of the program, when new tools, new plant facilities, new assembly lines, new shipways must first be constructed before the actual material begins to flow steadily and speedily from them.

The Congress of course, must rightly keep itself informed at all times of the progress of the program. However, there is certain information, as the Congress itself will readily recognize, which, in the interests of our own security and those of the nations that we are supporting, must of needs be kept in confidence.

New circumstances are constantly begetting new needs for our safety. I shall ask this Congress for greatly increased new appropriations and authorizations to carry on what we have begun.

I also ask this Congress for authority and for funds sufficient to manufacture additional munitions and war supplies of many kinds, to be turned over to those nations which are now in actual war with aggressor nations. Our most useful and immediate role is to act as an arsenal for them as well as for ourselves. They do not need manpower, but they do need billions of dollars' worth of the weapons of defense.

The time is near when they will not be able to pay for them all in ready cash. We cannot, and we will not, tell them that they must surrender merely because of present inability to pay for the weapons which we know they must have.

I do not recommend that we make them a loan of dollars with which to pay for these weapons–a loan to be repaid in dollars. I recommend that we make it possible for those nations to continue to obtain war materials in the United States, fitting their orders into our own program. And nearly all of their material would, if the time ever came, be useful in our own defense.

Taking counsel of expert military and naval authorities, considering what is best for our own security, we are free to decide how much should be kept here and how much should be sent abroad to our friends who, by their determined and heroic resistance, are giving us time in which to make ready our own defense.

For what we send abroad we shall be repaid, repaid within a reasonable time following the close of hostilities, repaid in similar materials, or at our option in other goods of many kinds which they can produce and which we need.

Let us say to the democracies: "We Americans are vitally concerned in your defense of freedom. We are putting forth our energies, our resources, and our organizing powers to give you the strength to regain and maintain a free world. We shall send you in ever-increasing numbers, ships, planes, tanks, guns. That is our purpose and our pledge."

In fulfillment of this purpose we will not be intimidated by the threats of dictators that they will regard as a breach of international law or as an act of war our aid to the democracies which dare to resist their aggression. Such aid–Such aid is not an act of war, even if a dictator should unilaterally proclaim it so to be.

And when the dictators–if the dictators–are ready to make war upon us, they will not wait for an act of war on our part.

They did not wait for Norway or Belgium or the Netherlands to commit an act of war. Their only interest is in a new one-way international law, which lacks mutuality in its observance and therefore becomes an instrument of oppression. The happiness of future generations of Americans may well depend on how effective and how immediate we can make our aid felt. No one can tell the exact character of the emergency situations that we may be called upon to meet. The nation's hands must not be tied when the nation's life is in danger.

Yes, and we must prepare, all of us prepare, to make the sacrifices that the emergency–almost as serious as war itself–demands. Whatever stands in the way of speed and efficiency in defense, in defense preparations of any kind, must give way to the national need.

A free nation has the right to expect full cooperation from all groups. A free nation has the right to look to the leaders of business, of labor, and of agriculture to take the lead in stimulating effort, not among other groups but within their own group.

The best way of dealing with the few slackers or trouble-makers in our midst is, first, to shame them by patriotic example, and if that fails, to use the sovereignty of government to save government.

As men do not live by bread alone, they do not fight by armaments alone. Those who man our defenses and those behind them who build our defenses must have the stamina and the courage which come from unshakable belief in the manner of life which they are defending. The mighty action that we are calling for cannot be based on a disregard of all the things worth fighting for.

The nation takes great satisfaction and much strength from the things which have been done to make its people conscious of their individual stake in the preservation of democratic life in America. Those things have toughened the fiber of our people, have renewed their faith and strengthened their devotion to the institutions we make ready to protect.

Certainly this is no time for any of us to stop thinking about the social and economic problems which are the root cause of the social revolution which is today a supreme factor in the world.

For there is nothing mysterious about the foundations of a healthy and strong democracy.

The basic things expected by our people of their political and economic systems are simple. They are:

Equality of opportunity for youth and for others.

Jobs for those who can work.

Security for those who need it.

The ending of special privilege for the few.

The preservation of civil liberties for all.

The enjoyment–The enjoyment of the fruits of scientific progress in a wider and constantly rising standard of living.

These are the simple, the basic things that must never be lost sight of in the turmoil and unbelievable complexity of our modern world. The inner and abiding strength of our economic and political systems is dependent upon the degree to which they fulfill these expectations.

Many subjects connected with our social economy call for immediate improvement. As examples:

We should bring more citizens under the coverage of old-age pensions and unemployment insurance.

We should widen the opportunities for adequate medical care.

We should plan a better system by which persons deserving or needing gainful employment may obtain it.

I have called for personal sacrifice, and I am assured of the willingness of almost all Americans to respond to that call. A part of the sacrifice means the payment of more money in taxes. In my budget message I will recommend that a greater portion of this great defense program be paid for from taxation than we are paying for today. No person should try, or be allowed to get rich out of the program, and the principle of tax payments in accordance with ability to pay should be constantly before our eyes to guide our legislation.

If the Congress maintains these principles the voters, putting patriotism ahead pocketbooks, will give you their applause.

In the future days, which we seek to make secure, we look forward to a world founded upon four essential human freedoms.

The first is freedom of speech and expression–everywhere in the world.

The second is freedom of every person to worship God in his own way everywhere in the world.

The third is freedom from want, which, translated into world terms, means economic understandings which will secure to every nation a healthy peacetime life for its inhabitants–everywhere in the world.

The fourth is freedom from fear, which, translated into world terms, means a world-wide reduction of armaments to such a point and in such a thorough fashion that no nation will be in a position to commit an act of physical aggression against any neighbor–anywhere in the world.

That is no vision of a distant millennium. It is a definite basis for a kind of world attainable in our own time and generation. That kind of world is the very antithesis of the so-called "new order" of tyranny which the dictators seek to create with the crash of a bomb.

To that new order we oppose the greater conception–the moral order. A good society is able to face schemes of world domination and foreign revolutions alike without fear.

Since the beginning of our American history we have been engaged in change, in a perpetual, peaceful revolution, a revolution which goes on steadily, quietly, adjusting itself to changing conditions without the concentration camp or the quicklime in the ditch. The world order which we seek is the cooperation of free countries, working together in a friendly, civilized society.

This nation has placed its destiny in the hands and heads and hearts of its millions of free men and women, and its faith in freedom under the guidance of God. Freedom means the supremacy of human rights everywhere. Our support goes to those who struggle to gain those rights and keep them. Our strength is our unity of purpose.

To that high concept there can be no end save victory.

■

Biographical Sketch: President George Walker Bush (born 6 July 1946) is the current President of the United States. His term is set to end on January 20, 2009. Eight months into Bush's first presidential term in 2001, the September 11, 2001 attacks on America occurred. Bush announced a 'war on terrorism', which became a central issue of his presidency. In early October 2001, he ordered the invasion of Afghanistan to overthrow the Taliban as part of an attempt to defeat al-Qaeda. He ordered the invasion of Iraq, in March 2003, asserting that Iraq was in violation of UN Resolution 1441 regarding weapons of mass destruction.

Speech By: President George W Bush

Topic: 9/11 speech - Address to the Nation

Date: September 11, 2001

Good evening. Today, our fellow citizens, our way of life, our very freedom came under attack in a series of deliberate and deadly terrorist acts. The victims were in airplanes, or in their offices; secretaries, businessmen and women, military and federal workers; moms and dads, friends and neighbors. Thousands of lives were suddenly ended by evil, despicable acts of terror.

The pictures of airplanes flying into buildings, fires burning, huge structures collapsing, have filled us with disbelief, terrible sadness, and a quiet, unyielding anger. These acts of mass murder were intended to frighten our nation into chaos and retreat. But they have failed; our country is strong.

A great people have been moved to defend a great nation. Terrorist attacks can shake the foundations of our biggest buildings, but they cannot touch the foundation of America. These acts shattered steel, but they cannot dent the steel of American resolve.

America was targeted for attack because we're the brightest beacon for freedom and opportunity in the world. And no one will keep that light from shining.

Today, our nation saw evil, the very worst of human nature. And we responded with the best of America–with the daring of our rescue workers, with the caring for strangers and neighbors who came to give blood and help in any way they could.

Immediately following the first attack, I implemented our government's emergency response plans. Our military is powerful, and it's prepared. Our emergency teams are working in New York City and Washington, D.C. to help with local rescue efforts.

Our first priority is to get help to those who have been injured, and to take every precaution to protect our citizens at home and around the world from further attacks.

The functions of our government continue without interruption. Federal agencies in Washington which had to be evacuated today are reopening for essential personnel tonight, and will be open for business tomorrow. Our financial institutions remain strong, and the American economy will be open for business, as well.

The search is underway for those who are behind these evil acts. I've directed the full resources of our intelligence and law enforcement communities to find those responsible and to bring them to justice. We will make no distinction between the terrorists who committed these acts and those who harbor them.

I appreciate so very much the members of Congress who have joined me in strongly condemning these attacks. And on behalf of the American people, I thank the many world leaders who have called to offer their condolences and assistance.

America and our friends and allies join with all those who want peace and security in the world, and we stand together to win the war against terrorism. Tonight, I ask for your prayers for all those who grieve, for the children whose worlds have been shattered, for all whose sense of safety and security has been threatened. And I pray they will be comforted by a power greater than any of us, spoken through the ages in Psalm 23: "Even though I walk through the valley of the shadow of death, I fear no evil, for You are with me."

This is a day when all Americans from every walk of life unite in our resolve for justice and peace. America has stood down enemies before, and we will do so this time. None of us will ever forget this day. Yet, we go forward to defend freedom and all that is good and just in our world.

Thank you. Good night, and God bless America.

■

Biographical Sketch: George Washington (February 22, 1732–December 14, 1799) was elected the first President of the United States of America in 1789. He led America's Continental Army to victory over Britain in the American Revolutionary War (1775–1783). In America, he is referred to as 'Father of the Nation' because of his central and critical role in the founding of the United States. His devotion to republicanism and civic virtue made him an exemplary figure among early American politicians.

Speech By: George Washington

Topic: Farewell Address to the People of the United States

Date: September 17, 1796

Friends and fellow-citizens:

The period for a new election of a citizen, to administer the executive government of the United States, being not far distant, and the time actually arrived, when your thoughts must be employed designating the person, who is to be clothed with that important trust, it appears to me proper, especially as it may conduce to a more distinct expression of the public voice, that I should now apprize you of the resolution I have formed, to decline being considered among the number of those out of whom a choice is to be made.

I beg you at the same time to do me the justice to be assured that this resolution has not been taken without a strict regard to all the considerations appertaining to the relation which binds a dutiful citizen to his country; and that in withdrawing the tender of service, which silence in my situation might imply, I am influenced by no diminution of zeal for your future interest, no deficiency of grateful respect for your past kindness, but am supported by a full conviction that the step is compatible with both.

The acceptance of, and continuance hitherto in, the office to which your suffrages have twice called me, have been a uniform sacrifice of inclination to the opinion of duty, and to a deference for what appeared to be your desire. I constantly hoped that it would have been much earlier in my power, consistently with motives, which I was not at liberty to disregard, to return to that retirement, from which I had been reluctantly drawn. The strength of my inclination to do this, previous to the last election, had even led to the preparation of an address to declare it to you; but mature reflection on the then perplexed and critical posture of our affairs with foreign nations, and the unanimous advice of persons entitled to my confidence impelled me to abandon the idea.

I rejoice, that the state of your concerns, external as well as internal, no longer renders the pursuit of inclination incompatible with the sentiment of duty, or propriety; and am persuaded, whatever partiality may be retained for my services, that, in the present circumstances of our country, you will not disapprove my determination to retire.

The impressions, with which I first undertook the arduous trust, were explained on the proper occasion. In the discharge of this trust, I will only say, that I have, with good intentions, contributed towards the organization and administration of the government the best exertions of which a very fallible judgment was capable. Not unconscious, in the outset, of the inferiority of my qualifications, experience in my own eyes, perhaps still more in the eyes of others, has strengthened the motives to diffidence of myself; and every day the increasing weight of years admonishes me more and more, that the shade of retirement is as necessary to me as it will be welcome. Satisfied, that, if any circumstances have given peculiar value to my services, they were temporary, I have the consolation to believe, that, while choice and prudence invite me to quit the political scene, patriotism does not forbid it.

In looking forward to the moment, which is intended to terminate the career of my public life, my feelings do not permit me to suspend the deep acknowledgment of that debt of gratitude, which I owe to my beloved country for the many honors it has conferred upon me; still more for the steadfast confidence with which it has supported me; and for the opportunities I have thence enjoyed of manifesting my inviolable attachment, by services faithful and persevering, though in usefulness unequal to my zeal. If benefits have resulted to our country from these services, let it always be remembered to your praise, and as an instructive example in our annals, that under circumstances in which the passions, agitated in every direction, were liable to mislead, amidst appearances sometimes dubious, vicissitudes of fortune often discouraging, in situations in which not unfrequently want of success has countenanced the spirit of criticism, the constancy of your support was the essential prop of the efforts, and a guarantee of the plans by which they were effected. Profoundly penetrated with this idea, I shall carry it with me to my grave, as a strong incitement to unceasing vows that Heaven may continue to you the choicest tokens of its beneficence; that your union and brotherly affection may be perpetual; that the free constitution, which is the work of your hands, may be sacredly maintained; that its administration in every department may be stamped with wisdom and virtue; than, in fine, the happiness of the people of these States, under the auspices of liberty, may be made complete, by so careful a preservation and so prudent a use of this blessing, as will acquire to them the glory of recommending it to the applause, the affection, and adoption of every nation, which is yet a stranger to it.

Here, perhaps I ought to stop. But a solicitude for your welfare which cannot end but with my life, and the apprehension of danger, natural to that solicitude, urge me, on an occasion like the present, to offer to your solemn contemplation, and to recommend to your frequent review, some sentiments which are the result of much reflection, of no inconsiderable observation, and which appear to me all-important to the permanency of your felicity as a people. These will be offered to you with the more freedom, as you can only see in them the disinterested warnings of a parting friend, who can possibly have no personal motive to bias his counsel. Nor can I forget, as an encouragement to it, your indulgent reception of my sentiments on a former and not dissimilar occasion.

Interwoven as is the love of liberty with every ligament of your hearts, no recommendation of mine is necessary to fortify or confirm the attachment.

The unity of Government, which constitutes you one people, is also now dear to you. It is justly so; for it is a main pillar in the edifice of your real independence, the support of your tranquility at home, your peace abroad; of your safety; of your prosperity; of that very Liberty, which you so highly prize. But as it is easy to foresee, that, from different causes and from different quarters, much pains will be taken, many artifices employed, to weaken in your minds the conviction of this truth; as this is the point in your political fortress against which the batteries of internal and external enemies will be most constantly and actively (though often covertly and insidiously) directed, it is of infinite moment, that you should properly estimate the immense value of your national Union to your collective and individual happiness; that you should cherish a cordial, habitual, and immovable attachment to it; accustoming yourselves to think and speak of it as of the Palladium of your political safety and prosperity; watching for its preservation with jealous anxiety; discountenancing whatever may suggest even a suspicion, that it can in any event be abandoned; and indignantly frowning upon the first dawning of every attempt to alienate any portion of our country from the rest, or to enfeeble the sacred ties which now link together the various parts.

For this you have every inducement of sympathy and interest. Citizens, by birth or choice, of a common country, that country has a right to concentrate your affections. The name of American, which belongs to you, in your national capacity, must always exalt the just pride of Patriotism, more than any appellation derived from local discriminations. With slight shades of difference, you have the same religion, manners, habits, and political principles. You have in a common cause fought and triumphed together; the Independence and Liberty you possess are the work of joint counsels, and joint efforts, of common dangers, sufferings, and successes.

But these considerations, however powerfully they address themselves to your sensibility, are greatly outweighed by those, which apply more immediately to your interest. Here every portion of our country finds the most commanding motives for carefully guarding and preserving the Union of the whole.

The North, in an unrestrained intercourse with the South, protected by the equal laws of a common government, finds, in the productions of the latter, great additional resources of maritime and commercial enterprise and precious materials of manufacturing industry. The South, in the same intercourse, benefiting by the agency of the North, sees its agriculture grow and its commerce expand. Turning partly into its own channels the seamen of the North, it finds its particular navigation invigorated; and, while it contributes, in different ways, to nourish and increase the general mass of the national navigation, it looks forward to the protection of a maritime strength, to which itself is unequally adapted. The East, in a like intercourse with the West, already finds, and in the progressive improvement of interior communications by land and water, will more and more find, a valuable vent for the commodities which it brings from abroad, or manufactures at home. The West derives from the East supplies requisite to its growth and comfort, and, what is perhaps of still greater consequence, it must of necessity owe the secure enjoyment of indispensable outlets for its own productions to the weight, influence, and the future maritime strength of the Atlantic side of the Union, directed by an indissoluble community of interest as one nation. Any other tenure by which the West can hold this essential advantage, whether derived from its own separate strength, or from an apostate and unnatural connexion with any foreign power, must be intrinsically precarious.

While, then, every part of our country thus feels an immediate and particular interest in Union, all the parts combined cannot fail to find in the united mass of means and efforts greater strength, greater resource, proportionably greater security from external danger, a less frequent interruption of their peace by foreign nations; and, what is of inestimable value, they must derive from Union an exemption from those broils and wars between themselves, which so frequently afflict neighbouring countries not tied together by the same governments, which their own rivalships alone would be sufficient to produce, but which opposite foreign alliances, attachments, and intrigues would stimulate and embitter. Hence, likewise, they will avoid the necessity of those overgrown military establishments, which, under any form of government, are inauspicious to liberty, and which are to be regarded as particularly hostile to Republican Liberty. In this sense it is, that your Union ought to be considered as a main prop of your liberty, and that the love of the one ought to endear to you the preservation of the other.

These considerations speak a persuasive language to every reflecting and virtuous mind, and exhibit the continuance of the union as a primary object of Patriotic desire. Is there a doubt, whether a common government can embrace so large a sphere? Let experience solve it. To listen to mere speculation in such a case were criminal. We are authorized to hope, that a proper organization of the whole, with the auxiliary agency of governments for the respective subdivisions, will afford a happy issue to the experiment. It is well worth a fair and full experiment. With such powerful and obvious motives to Union, affecting all parts of our country, while experience shall not have demonstrated its impracticability, there will always be reason to distrust the patriotism of those, who in any quarter may endeavour to weaken its bands.

In contemplating the causes, which may disturb our Union, it occurs as matter of serious concern, that any ground should have been furnished for characterizing parties by Geographical discriminations, Northern and Southern, Atlantic and Western; whence designing men may endeavour to excite a belief, that there is a real difference of local interests and views. One of the expedients of party to acquire influence, within particular districts, is to misrepresent the opinions and aims of other districts. You cannot shield yourselves too much against the jealousies and heart-burnings, which spring from these misrepresentations; they tend to render alien to each other those, who ought to be bound together by fraternal affection. The inhabitants of our western country have lately had a useful lesson on this head; they have seen, in the negotiation by the Executive, and in the unanimous ratification by the Senate, of the treaty with Spain, and in the universal satisfaction at that event, throughout the United States, a decisive proof how unfounded were the suspicions propagated among them of a policy in the General Government and in the Atlantic States unfriendly to their interests in regard to the Mississippi; they have been witnesses to the formation of two treaties, that with Great Britain, and that with Spain, which secure to them every thing they could desire, in respect to our foreign relations, towards confirming their prosperity. Will it not be their wisdom to rely for the preservation of these advantages on the union by which they were procured? Will they not henceforth be deaf to those advisers, if such there are, who would sever them from their brethren, and connect them with aliens?

To the efficacy and permanency of your Union, a Government for the whole is indispensable. No alliances, however strict, between the parts can be an adequate substitute; they must inevitably experience the infractions and interruptions, which all alliances in all times have experienced. Sensible of this momentous truth, you have improved upon your first essay, by the adoption of a Constitution of Government better calculated than your former for an intimate Union, and for the efficacious management of your common concerns. This Government, the offspring of our own choice, uninfluenced and unawed, adopted upon full investigation and mature deliberation, completely free in its principles, in the distribution of its powers, uniting security with energy, and containing within itself a provision for its own amendment, has a just claim to your confidence and your support. Respect for its authority, compliance with its laws, acquiescence in its measures, are duties enjoined by the fundamental maxims of true Liberty. The basis of our political systems is the right of the people to make and to alter their Constitutions of Government. But the Constitution which at any time exists, till changed by an explicit and authentic act of the whole people, is sacredly obligatory upon all. The very idea of the power and the right of the people to establish Government presupposes the duty of every individual to obey the established Government.

All obstructions to the execution of the Laws, all combinations and associations, under whatever plausible character, with the real design to direct, control, counteract, or awe the regular deliberation and action of the constituted authorities, are destructive of this fundamental principle, and of fatal tendency. They serve to organize faction, to give it an artificial and extraordinary force; to put, in the place of the delegated will of the nation, the will of a party, often a small but artful and enterprising minority of the community; and, according to the alternate triumphs of different parties, to make the public administration the mirror of the ill-concerted and incongruous projects of faction, rather than the organ of consistent and wholesome plans digested by common counsels, and modified by mutual interests.

However combinations or associations of the above description may now and then answer popular ends, they are likely, in the course of time and things, to become potent engines, by which cunning, ambitious, and unprincipled men will be enabled to subvert the power of the people, and to usurp for themselves the reins of government; destroying afterwards the very engines, which have lifted them to unjust dominion.

Towards the preservation of your government, and the permanency of your present happy state, it is requisite, not only that you steadily discountenance irregular oppositions to its acknowledged authority, but also that you resist with care the spirit of innovation upon its principles, however specious the pretexts. One method of assault may be to effect, in the forms of the constitution, alterations, which will impair the energy of the system, and thus to undermine what cannot be directly overthrown. In all the changes to which you may be invited, remember that time and habit are at least as necessary to fix the true character of governments, as of other human institutions; that experience is the surest standard, by which to test the real tendency of the existing constitution of a country; that facility in changes, upon the credit of mere hypothesis and opinion, exposes to perpetual change, from the endless variety of hypothesis and opinion; and remember, especially, that, for the efficient management of our common interests, in a country so extensive as ours, a government of as much vigor as is consistent with the perfect security of liberty is indispensable. Liberty itself will find in such a government, with powers properly distributed and adjusted, its surest guardian. It is, indeed, little else than a name, where the government is too feeble to withstand the enterprises of faction, to confine each member of the society within the limits prescribed by the laws, and to maintain all in the secure and tranquil enjoyment of the rights of person and property.

I have already intimated to you the danger of parties in the state, with particular reference to the founding of them on geographical discriminations. Let me now take a more comprehensive view, and warn you in the most solemn manner against the baneful effects of the spirit of party, generally.

This spirit, unfortunately, is inseparable from our nature, having its root in the strongest passions of the human mind. It exists under different shapes in all governments, more or less stifled, controlled, or repressed; but, in those of the popular form, it is seen in its greatest rankness, and is truly their worst enemy.

The alternate domination of one faction over another, sharpened by the spirit of revenge, natural to party dissension, which in different ages and countries has perpetrated the most horrid enormities, is itself a frightful despotism. But this leads at length to a more formal and permanent despotism. The disorders and miseries, which result, gradually incline the minds of men to seek security and repose in the absolute power of an individual; and sooner or later the chief of some prevailing faction, more able or more fortunate than his competitors, turns this disposition to the purposes of his own elevation, on the ruins of Public Liberty.

Without looking forward to an extremity of this kind, (which nevertheless ought not to be entirely out of sight,) the common and continual mischiefs of the spirit of party are sufficient to make it the interest and duty of a wise people to discourage and restrain it.

It serves always to distract the Public Councils, and enfeeble the Public Administration. It agitates the Community with ill-founded jealousies and false alarms; kindles the animosity of one part against another, foments occasionally riot and insurrection. It opens the door to foreign influence and corruption, which find a facilitated access to the government itself through the channels of party passions. Thus the policy and the will of one country are subjected to the policy and will of another.

There is an opinion, that parties in free countries are useful checks upon the administration of the Government, and serve to keep alive the spirit of Liberty. This within certain limits is probably true; and in Governments of a Monarchical cast, Patriotism may look with indulgence, if not with favor, upon the spirit of party. But in those of the popular character, in Governments purely elective, it is a spirit not to be encouraged. From their natural tendency, it is certain there will always be enough of that spirit for every salutary purpose. And, there being constant danger of excess, the effort ought to be, by force of public opinion, to mitigate and assuage it. A fire not to be quenched, it demands a uniform vigilance to prevent its bursting into a flame, lest, instead of warming, it should consume.

It is important, likewise, that the habits of thinking in a free country should inspire caution, in those entrusted with its administration, to confine themselves within their respective constitutional spheres, avoiding in the exercise of the powers of one department to encroach upon another. The spirit of encroachment tends to consolidate the powers of all the departments in one, and thus to create, whatever the form of government, a real despotism. A just estimate of that love of power, and proneness to abuse it, which predominates in the human heart, is sufficient to satisfy us of the truth of this position. The necessity of reciprocal checks in the exercise of political power, by dividing and distributing it into different depositories, and constituting each the Guardian of the Public Weal against invasions by the others, has been evinced by experiments ancient and modern; some of them in our country and under our own eyes. To preserve them must be as necessary as to institute them. If, in the opinion of the people, the distribution or modification of the constitutional powers be in any particular wrong, let it be corrected by an amendment in the way, which the constitution designates. But let there be no change by usurpation; for, though this, in one instance, may be the instrument of good, it is the customary weapon by which free governments are destroyed. The precedent must always greatly overbalance in permanent evil any partial or transient benefit, which the use can at any time yield.

Of all the dispositions and habits, which lead to political prosperity, Religion and Morality are indispensable supports. In vain would that man claim the tribute of Patriotism, who should labor to subvert these great pillars of human happiness, these firmest props of the duties of Men and Citizens. The mere Politician, equally with the pious man, ought to respect and to cherish them. A volume could not trace all their connexions with private and public felicity. Let it simply be asked, Where is the security for property, for reputation, for life, if the sense of religious obligation desert the oaths, which are the instruments of investigation in Courts of Justice? And let us with caution indulge the supposition, that morality can be maintained without religion. Whatever may be conceded to the influence of refined education on minds of peculiar structure, reason and experience both forbid us to expect, that national morality can prevail in exclusion of religious principle.

It is substantially true, that virtue or morality is a necessary spring of popular government. The rule, indeed, extends with more or less force to every species of free government. Who, that is a sincere friend to it, can look with indifference upon attempts to shake the foundation of the fabric?

Promote, then, as an object of primary importance, institutions for the general diffusion of knowledge. In proportion as the structure of a government gives force to public opinion, it is essential that public opinion should be enlightened.

As a very important source of strength and security, cherish public credit. One method of preserving it is, to use it as sparingly as possible; avoiding occasions of expense by cultivating peace, but remembering also that timely disbursements to prepare for danger frequently prevent much greater disbursements to repel it; avoiding likewise the accumulation of debt, not only by shunning occasions of expense, but by vigorous exertions in time of peace to discharge the debts, which unavoidable wars may have occasioned, not ungenerously throwing upon posterity the burthen, which we ourselves ought to bear. The execution of these maxims belongs to your representatives, but it is necessary that public opinion should cooperate. To facilitate to them the performance of their duty, it is essential that you should practically bear in mind, that towards the payment of debts there must be Revenue; that to have Revenue there must be taxes; that no taxes can be devised, which are not more or less inconvenient and unpleasant; that the intrinsic embarrassment, inseparable from the selection of the proper objects (which is always a choice of difficulties), ought to be a decisive motive for a candid construction of the conduct of the government in making it, and for a spirit of acquiescence in the measures for obtaining revenue, which the public exigencies may at any time dictate.

Observe good faith and justice towards all Nations; cultivate peace and harmony with all. Religion and Morality enjoin this conduct; and can it be, that good policy does not equally enjoin it? It will be worthy of a free, enlightened, and, at no distant period, a great Nation, to give to mankind the magnanimous and too novel example of a people always guided by an exalted justice and benevolence. Who can doubt, that, in the course of time and things, the fruits of such a plan would richly repay any temporary advantages, which might be lost by a steady adherence to it ? Can it be, that Providence has not connected the permanent felicity of a Nation with its Virtue? The experiment, at least, is recommended by every sentiment which ennobles human nature. Alas! is it rendered impossible by its vices?

In the execution of such a plan, nothing is more essential, than that permanent, inveterate antipathies against particular Nations, and passionate attachments for others, should be excluded; and that, in place of them, just and amicable feelings towards all should be cultivated. The Nation, which indulges towards another an habitual hatred, or an habitual fondness, is in some degree a slave. It is a slave to its animosity or to its affection, either of which is sufficient to lead it astray from its duty and its interest. Antipathy in one nation against another disposes each more readily to offer insult and injury, to lay hold of slight causes of umbrage, and to be haughty and intractable, when accidental or trifling occasions of dispute occur. Hence frequent collisions, obstinate, envenomed, and bloody contests. The Nation, prompted by ill-will and resentment, sometimes impels to war the Government, contrary to the best calculations of policy. The Government sometimes participates in the national propensity, and adopts through passion what reason would reject; at other times, it makes the animosity of the nation subservient to projects of hostility instigated by pride, ambition, and other sinister and pernicious motives. The peace often, sometimes perhaps the liberty, of Nations has been the victim.

So likewise, a passionate attachment of one Nation for another produces a variety of evils. Sympathy for the favorite Nation, facilitating the illusion of an imaginary common interest, in cases where no real common interest exists, and infusing into one the enmities of the other, betrays the former into a participation in the quarrels and wars of the latter, without adequate inducement or justification. It leads also to concessions to the favorite Nation of privileges denied to others, which is apt doubly to injure the Nation making the concessions; by unnecessarily parting with what ought to have been retained; and by exciting jealousy, ill-will, and a disposition to retaliate, in the parties from whom equal privileges are withheld. And it gives to ambitious, corrupted, or deluded citizens, (who devote themselves to the favorite nation,) facility to betray or sacrifice the interests of their own country, without odium, sometimes even with popularity; gilding, with the appearances of a virtuous sense of obligation, a commendable deference for public opinion, or a laudable zeal for public good, the base or foolish compliances of ambition, corruption, or infatuation. As avenues to foreign influence in innumerable ways, such attachments are particularly alarming to the truly enlightened and independent Patriot. How many opportunities do they afford to tamper with domestic factions, to practise the arts of seduction, to mislead public opinion, to influence or awe the Public Councils! Such an attachment of a small or weak, towards a great and powerful nation, dooms the former to be the satellite of the latter.

Against the insidious wiles of foreign influence (I conjure you to believe me, fellow-citizens,) the jealousy of a free people ought to be constantly awake; since history and experience prove, that foreign influence is one of the most baneful foes of Republican Government. But that jealousy, to be useful, must be impartial; else it becomes the instrument of the very influence to be avoided, instead of a defence against it. Excessive partiality for one foreign nation, and excessive dislike of another, cause those whom they actuate to see danger only on one side, and serve to veil and even second the arts of influence on the other. Real patriots, who may resist the intrigues of the favorite, are liable to become suspected and odious; while its tools and dupes usurp the applause and confidence of the people, to surrender their interests.

The great rule of conduct for us, in regard to foreign nations, is, in extending our commercial relations, to have with them as little political connexion as possible. So far as we have already formed engagements, let them be fulfilled with perfect good faith. Here let us stop. Europe has a set of primary interests, which to us have none, or a very remote relation. Hence she must be engaged in frequent controversies, the causes of which are essentially foreign to our concerns. Hence, therefore, it must be unwise in us to implicate ourselves, by artificial ties, in the ordinary vicissitudes of her politics, or the ordinary combinations and collisions of her friendships or enmities.

Our detached and distant situation invites and enables us to pursue a different course. If we remain one people, under an efficient government, the period is not far off, when we may defy material injury from external annoyance; when we may take such an attitude as will cause the neutrality, we may at any time resolve upon, to be scrupulously respected; when belligerent nations, under the impossibility of making acquisitions upon us, will not lightly hazard the giving us provocation; when we may choose peace or war, as our interest, guided by justice, shall counsel.

Why forego the advantages of so peculiar a situation? Why quit our own to stand upon foreign ground? Why, by interweaving our destiny with that of any part of Europe, entangle our peace and prosperity in the toils of European ambition, rivalship, interest, humor, or caprice?

It is our true policy to steer clear of permanent alliances with any portion of the foreign world; so far, I mean, as we are now at liberty to do it; for let me not be understood as capable of patronizing infidelity to existing engagements. I hold the maxim no less applicable to public than to private affairs, that honesty is always the best policy. I repeat it, therefore, let those engagements be observed in their genuine sense. But, in my opinion, it is unnecessary and would be unwise to extend them.

Taking care always to keep ourselves, by suitable establishments, on a respectable defensive posture, we may safely trust to temporary alliances for extraordinary emergencies.

Harmony, liberal intercourse with all nations, are recommended by policy, humanity, and interest. But even our commercial policy should hold an equal and impartial hand; neither seeking nor granting exclusive favors or preferences; consulting the natural course of things; diffusing and diversifying by gentle means the streams of commerce, but forcing nothing; establishing, with powers so disposed, in order to give trade a stable course, to define the rights of our merchants, and to enable the government to support them, conventional rules of intercourse, the best that present circumstances and mutual opinion will permit, but temporary, and liable to be from time to time abandoned or varied, as experience and circumstances shall dictate; constantly keeping in view, that it is folly in one nation to look for disinterested favors from another; that it must pay with a portion of its independence for whatever it may accept under that character; that, by such acceptance, it may place itself in the condition of having given equivalents for nominal favors, and yet of being reproached with ingratitude for not giving more. There can be no greater error than to expect or calculate upon real favors from nation to nation. It is an illusion, which experience must cure, which a just pride ought to discard.

In offering to you, my countrymen, these counsels of an old and affectionate friend, I dare not hope they will make the strong and lasting impression I could wish; that they will control the usual current of the passions, or prevent our nation from running the course, which has hitherto marked the destiny of nations. But, if I may even flatter myself, that they may be productive of some partial benefit, some occasional good; that they may now and then recur to moderate the fury of party spirit, to warn against the mischiefs of foreign intrigue, to guard against the impostures of pretended patriotism; this hope will be a full recompense for the solicitude for your welfare, by which they have been dictated.

How far in the discharge of my official duties, I have been guided by the principles which have been delineated, the public records and other evidences of my conduct must witness to you and to the world. To myself, the assurance of my own conscience is, that I have at least believed myself to be guided by them.

In relation to the still subsisting war in Europe, my Proclamation of the 22nd of April 1793, is the index to my Plan. Sanctioned by your approving voice, and by that of your Representatives in both Houses of Congress, the spirit of that measure has continually governed me, uninfluenced by any attempts to deter or divert me from it.

After deliberate examination, with the aid of the best lights I could obtain, I was well satisfied that our country, under all the circumstances of the case, had a right to take, and was bound in duty and interest to take, a neutral position. Having taken it, I determined, as far as should depend upon me, to maintain it, with moderation, perseverance, and firmness.

The considerations, which respect the right to hold this conduct, it is not necessary on this occasion to detail. I will only observe, that, according to my understanding of the matter, that right, so far from being denied by any of the Belligerent Powers, has been virtually admitted by all.

The duty of holding a neutral conduct may be inferred, without any thing more, from the obligation which justice and humanity impose on every nation, in cases in which it is free to act, to maintain inviolate the relations of peace and amity towards other nations. The inducements of interest for observing that conduct will best be referred to your own reflections and experience. With me, a predominant motive has been to endeavour to gain time to our country to settle and mature its yet recent institutions, and to progress without interruption to that degree of strength and consistency, which is necessary to give it, humanly speaking, the command of its own fortunes.

Though, in reviewing the incidents of my administration, I am unconscious of intentional error, I am nevertheless too sensible of my defects not to think it probable that I may have committed many errors. Whatever they may be, I fervently beseech the Almighty to avert or mitigate the evils to which they may tend. I shall also carry with me the hope, that my Country will never cease to view them with indulgence; and that, after forty-five years of my life dedicated to its service with an upright zeal, the faults of incompetent abilities will be consigned to oblivion, as myself must soon be to the mansions of rest.

Relying on its kindness in this as in other things, and actuated by that fervent love towards it, which is so natural to a man, who views it in the native soil of himself and his progenitors for several generations; I anticipate with pleasing expectation that retreat, in which I promise myself to realize, without alloy, the sweet enjoyment of partaking, in the midst of my fellow-citizens, the benign influence of good laws under a free government, the ever favorite object of my heart, and the happy reward, as I trust, of our mutual cares, labors, and dangers.

■

Biographical Sketch: Hillary Diane Rodham Clinton (born October 26, 1947) is the junior United States Senator from New York. She is a member of the Democratic Party. She is married to Bill Clinton, the 42nd President of the United States. She was elected to the United States Senate in 2000. She became the first First, Lady elected to public office and the first female senator to represent New York. In 2006, she was re-elected.

Speech By: Hillary Clinton

Topic: Women's Rights are Human Rights

Date: September 5, 1995

Mrs. Mongella, Under Secretary Kittani, distinguished delegates and guests:

I would like to thank the Secretary General of the United Nations for inviting me to be part of the United Nations Fourth World Conference on Women. This is truly a celebration–a celebration of the contributions women make in every aspect of life: in the home, on the job, in their communities, as mothers, wives, sisters, daughters, learners, workers, citizens and leaders.

It is also a coming together, much the way women come together every day in every country.

We come together in fields and in factories. In village markets and supermarkets. In living rooms and board rooms.

Whether it is while playing with our children in the park, or washing clothes in a river, or taking a break at the office water cooler, we come together and talk about our aspirations and concerns. And time and again, our talk turns to our children and our families. However different we may be, there is far more that unites us than divides us. We share a common future. And we are here to find common ground so that we may help bring new dignity and respect to women and girls all over the world–and in so doing, bring new strength and stability to families as well.

By gathering in Beijing, we are focusing world attention on issues that matter most in the lives of women and their families: access to education, health care, jobs and credit, the chance to enjoy basic legal and human rights and participate fully in the political life of their countries.

There are some who question the reason for this conference.

Let them listen to the voices of women in their homes, neighborhoods, and workplaces.

There are some who wonder whether the lives of women and girls matter to economic and political progress around the globe.

Let them look at the women gathered here and at Huairou–the homemakers, nurses, teachers, lawyers, policymakers, and women who run their own businesses.

It is conferences like this that compel governments and people everywhere to listen, look and face the world's most pressing problems.

Wasn't it after the women's conference in Nairobi ten years ago that the world focused for the first time on the crisis of domestic violence?

Earlier today, I participated in a World Health Organization forum, where government officials, NGOs, and individual citizens are working on ways to address the health problems of women and girls.

Tomorrow, I will attend a gathering of the United Nations Development Fund for Women. There, the discussion will focus on local–and highly successful–programs that give hard-working women access to credit so they can improve their own lives and the lives of their families.

What we are learning around the world is that if women are healthy and educated, their families will flourish. If women are free from violence, their families will flourish. If women have a chance to work and earn as full and equal partners in society, their families will flourish.

And when families flourish, communities and nations will flourish.

That is why every woman, every man, every child, every family, and every nation on our planet has a stake in the discussion that takes place here.

Over the past 25 years, I have worked persistently on issues relating to women, children and families. Over the past two-and-a-half years, I have had the opportunity to learn more about the challenges facing women in my own country and around the world.

I have met new mothers in Jojakarta, Indonesia, who come together regularly in their village to discuss nutrition, family planning, and baby care.

I have met working parents in Denmark who talk about the comfort they feel in knowing that their children can be cared for in creative, safe, and nurturing after-school centers.

I have met women in South Africa who helped lead the struggle to end apartheid and are now helping build a new democracy.

I have met with the leading women of the Western Hemisphere who are working every day to promote literacy and better health care for the children of their countries.

I have met women in India and Bangladesh who are taking out small loans to buy milk cows, rickshaws, thread and other materials to create a livelihood for themselves and their families.

I have met doctors and nurses in Belarus and Ukraine who are trying to keep children alive in the aftermath of Chernobyl.

The great challenge of this Conference is to give voice to women everywhere whose experiences go unnoticed, whose words go unheard.

Women comprise more than half the world's population. Women are 70 per cent of the world's poor, and two-thirds of those who are not taught to read and write.

Women are the primary caretakers for most of the world's children and elderly. Yet much of the work we do is not valued–not by economists, not by historians, not by popular culture, not by government leaders.

At this very moment, as we sit here, women around the world are giving birth, raising children, cooking meals, washing clothes, cleaning houses, planting crops, working on assembly lines, running companies, and running countries.

Women also are dying from diseases that should have been prevented or treated; they are watching their children succumb to malnutrition caused by poverty and economic deprivation; they are being denied the right to go to school by their own fathers and brothers; they are being forced into prostitution, and they are being barred from the bank lending office and banned from the ballot box.

Those of us who have the opportunity to be here have the responsibility to speak for those who could not.

As an American, I want to speak up for women in my own country–women who are raising children on the minimum wage, women who can't afford health care or child care, women whose lives are threatened by violence, including violence in their own homes.

I want to speak up for mothers who are fighting for good schools, safe neighborhoods, clean air and clean airwaves; for older women, some of them widows, who have raised their families and now find that their skills and life experiences are not valued in the workplace; for women who are working all night as nurses, hotel clerks, and fast food cooks so that they can be at home during the day with their kids; and for women everywhere who simply don't have time to do everything they are called upon to do each day.

Speaking to you today, I speak for them, just as each of us speaks for women around the world who are denied the chance to go to school, or see a doctor, or own property, or have a say about the direction of their lives, simply because they are women. The truth is that most women around the world work both inside and outside the home, usually by necessity.

We need to understand that there is no formula for how women should lead their lives. That is why we must respect the choices that each woman makes for herself and her family. Every woman deserves the chance to realize her God-given potential.

We also must recognize that women will never gain full dignity until their human rights are respected and protected.

Our goals for this Conference, to strengthen families and societies by empowering women to take greater control over their own destinies, cannot be fully achieved unless all governments–here and around the world–accept their responsibility to protect and promote internationally recognized human rights.

The international community has long acknowledged - and recently affirmed at Vienna–that both women and men are entitled to a range of protections and personal freedoms, from the right of personal security to the right to determine freely the number and spacing of the children they bear.

No one should be forced to remain silent for fear of religious or political persecution, arrest, abuse or torture.

Tragically, women are most often the ones whose human rights are violated.

Even in the late 20th century, the rape of women continues to be used as an instrument of armed conflict. Women and children make up a large majority of the world's refugees. When women are excluded from the political process, they become even more vulnerable to abuse.

I believe that, on the eve of a new millennium, it is time to break our silence. It is time for us to say here in Beijing, and the world to hear, that it is no longer acceptable to discuss women's rights as separate from human rights.

These abuses have continued because, for too long, the history of women has been a history of silence. Even today, there are those who are trying to silence our words.

The voices of this conference and of the women at Huairou must be heard loud and clear: It is a violation of human rights when babies are denied food, or drowned, or suffocated, or their spines broken, simply because they are born girls.

It is a violation of human rights when women and girls are sold into the slavery of prostitution.

It is a violation of human rights when women are doused with gasoline, set on fire and burned to death because their marriage dowries are deemed too small.

It is a violation of human rights when individual women are raped in their own communities and when thousands of women are subjected to rape as a tactic or prize of war.

It is a violation of human rights when a leading cause of death worldwide among women ages 14 to 44 is the violence they are subjected to in their own homes.

It is a violation of human rights when young girls are brutalized by the painful and degrading practice of genital mutilation.

It is a violation of human rights when women are denied the right to plan their own families, and that includes being forced to have abortions or being sterilized against their will.

If there is one message that echoes forth from this conference, it is that human rights are women's rights–and women's rights are human rights. Let us not forget that among those rights are the right to speak freely–and the right to be heard.

Women must enjoy the right to participate fully in the social and political lives of their countries if we want freedom and democracy to thrive and endure.

It is indefensible that many women in nongovernmental organizations who wished to participate in this conference have not been able to attend - or have been prohibited from fully taking part.

Let me be clear. Freedom means the right of people to assemble, organize, and debate openly. It means respecting the views of those who may disagree with the views of their governments. It means not taking citizens away from their loved ones and jailing them, mistreating them, or denying them their freedom or dignity because of the peaceful expression of their ideas and opinions.

In my country, we recently celebrated the 75th anniversary of women's suffrage. It took 150 years after the signing of our Declaration of Independence for women to win the right to vote.

It took 72 years of organized struggle on the part of many courageous women and men. It was one of America's most divisive philosophical wars. But it was also a bloodless war. Suffrage was achieved without a shot being fired.

We have also been reminded, in V-1 Day observances last weekend, of the good that comes when men and women join together to combat the forces of tyranny and build a better world.

We have seen peace prevail in most places for a half century. We have avoided another world war.

But we have not solved older, deeply-rooted problems that continue to diminish the potential of half the world's population.

Now it is time to act on behalf of women everywhere. If we take bold steps to better the lives of women, we will be taking bold steps to better the lives of children and families too.

Families rely on mothers and wives for emotional support and care; families rely on women for labor in the home; and increasingly, families rely on women for income needed to raise healthy children and care for other relatives.

As long as discrimination and inequities remain so commonplace around the world - as long as girls and women are valued less, fed less, fed last, overworked, underpaid, not schooled and subjected to violence in and out of their homes - the potential of the human family to create a peaceful, prosperous world will not be realized.

Let this Conference be our–and the world's–call to action.

And let us heed the call so that we can create a world in which every woman is treated with respect and dignity, every boy and girl is loved and cared for equally, and every family has the hope of a strong and stable future.

Thank you very much.

God's blessings on you, your work and all who will benefit from it.

■

Biographical Sketch: Indira Priyadarshini Gandhi (November 19, 1917 – October 31, 1984) was India's first woman Prime Minister from January 19, 1966 to March 24, 1977, and again from January 14, 1980 until her assassination on October 31, 1984. She was the daughter of India's first Prime Minister, Jawaharlal Nehru, and mother of Rajiv Gandhi. Her charm, intelligence and charisma made her a powerful statesperson, much loved and admired by her people. Economically, she led India to become one of the fastest growing economies in the world.

Speech By: Indira Gandhi

Topic: Martin Luther King

Date: January 24, 1969

This is a poignant moment for all of us. We remember vividly your last visit to our country. We had hoped that on this occasion, Dr. King and you would be standing side by side on this platform. That was not to be. He is not with us but we feel his spirit. We admired Dr. King. We felt his loss as our own. The tragedy rekindled memories of the great martyrs of all time who gave their lives so that men might live and grow. We thought of the great men in your own country who fell to the assassin's bullet and of Mahatma Gandhi's martyrdom here in this city, this very month, twenty-one years ago. Such events remain as wounds in the human consciousness, reminding us of battles, yet to be fought and tasks still to be accomplished. We should not mourn for men of high ideals. Rather we should rejoice that we had the privilege of having had them with us, to inspire us by their radiant personalities. So today, we are gathered not to offer you grief, but to salute a man who achieved so much in so short a time. It is befitting, Madam, that you whom he called the 'courage by my side', you who gave him strength and encouragement in his historic mission, should be with us to receive this award.

You and your husband both had foreseen that death might come to him violently. It was perhaps inherent in the situation. Dr. King chose death for the theme of a sermon, remarking that he would like to be remembered as a drum major for justice, for peace and for righteousness. When you were once asked what you would do if your husband were assassinated, you were courage personified, replying that you might weep but the work would go on. Your face of sorrow, so beautiful in its dignity coupled with infinite compassion, will forever be engraved in our hearts.

Mahatma Gandhi also had foreseen his end and had prepared himself for it. Just as training for violence included learning to kill, the training for non-violence, he said, included learning how to die. The true badge of the satyagrahi is to be unafraid.

As if he too had envisaged the martyrdoms of Mahatma Gandhi and Martin Luther King, Rabindranath Tagore once sang:

In anger we slew him,

With love let us embrace him now,

For in death he lives again amongst us,

The mighty conqueror of death.

This award, Madam, is the highest tribute our nation can bestow on work for understanding and brotherhood among men. It is named after a man who himself was a peace-maker and who all his life laboured passionately for freedom, justice and peace in

India and throughout the world. Dr. Martin Luther King's struggle was for these same values. He paid for his ideals with his blood, forging a new bond among the brave and the conscientious of all races and all nations.

Dr. King's dream embraced the poor and the oppressed of all lands. His work ennobled us. He spoke of the right of man to survive and recognized three threats to the survival of man—racial injustice, poverty and war. He realised that even under the lamp of affluence which was held aloft by science, lay the shadow of poverty, compelling two-thirds of the peoples of the world to exist in hunger and want. He proclaimed that mankind could be saved from war only if we cared enough for peace to sacrifice for it.

Dr. Martin Luther King drew his inspiration from Christ, and his method of action from Mahatma Gandhi. Only through truth can untruth be vanquished. Only through love can hatred be quenched. This is the path of the Buddha and of Christ, and in our own times, that of Mahatma Gandhi and of Martin Luther King.

They believed in the equality of all men. No more false doctrine has been spread than that of the superiority of one race over another. It is ironical that there should still be people in this world who judge men not by their moral worth and intellectual merit but by the pigment of their skin or other physical characteristics.

Some governments still rest on the theory of racist superiority—such as the governments of South Africa and the lawless regime in Rhodesia. Unregenerate groups in other countries consider one colour superior to another. Our own battle is not yet over. Caste and other prejudices still survive, but most of us are ashamed of them and recognise them as evils to be combated. We are trying hard to eradicate them.

While there is bondage anywhere, we ourselves cannot be fully free. While there is oppression anywhere, we ourselves cannot soar high. Martin Luther King was convinced that one day the misguided people who believed in racial superiority would realise the error of their ways. His dream was that white and black, brown and yellow would live and grow together as flowers in a garden with their faces turned towards the sun. As you yourself said, 'All of us who believe in what Martin Luther King stood for, must see to it that his spirit never dies'. That spirit can never die. There may be setbacks in our fight for the equality of all men. There may be moments of gloom. But victory must and will be ours. Let us not rest until the equality of all races and religions becomes a living fact. That is the most effective and lasting tribute that we can pay to Dr. King.

■

Biographical Sketch: Jawaharlal Nehru (November 14, 1889–May 27, 1964) was the leader of the Indian National Congress. He was a pivotal figure during the Indian independence movement. After India gained independence from the British rule, he served as the first Prime Minister of the Republic of India. Apart from being a leader and a politician, he was also a writer, scholar and an amateur historian. Under his rule, India experienced major phases of industrialisation, agrarian and land reforms, infrastructure and energy development. Nehru passionately worked for women's rights, secularism and advancement of education and social welfare.

Speech By: Jawaharlal Nehru

Topic: Speech on the Granting of Indian Independence

Date: August 14, 1947

Long years ago we made a tryst with destiny, and now the time comes when we shall redeem our pledge, not wholly or in full measure, but very substantially. At the stroke of the midnight hour, when the world sleeps, India will awake to life and freedom. A moment comes, which comes but rarely in history, when we step out from the old to the new, when an age ends, and when the soul of a nation, long suppressed, finds utterance. It is fitting that at this solemn moment we take the pledge of dedication to the service of India and her people and to the still larger cause of humanity.

At the dawn of history India started on her unending quest, and trackless centuries are filled with her striving and the grandeur of her success and her failures. Through good and ill fortune alike she has never lost sight of that quest or forgotten the ideals which gave her strength. We end today a period of ill fortune and India discovers herself again. The achievement we celebrate today is but a step, an opening of opportunity, to the greater triumphs and achievements that await us. Are we brave enough and wise enough to grasp this opportunity and accept the challenge of the future?

Freedom and power bring responsibility. The responsibility rests upon this Assembly, a sovereign body representing the sovereign people of India. Before the birth of freedom we have endured all the pains of labour and our hearts are heavy with the memory of this sorrow. Some of those pains continue even now. Nevertheless, the past is over and it is the future that beckons to us now.

That future is not one of ease or resting but of incessant striving so that we may fulfil the pledges we have so often taken and the one we shall take today. The service of India means the service of the millions who suffer. It means the ending of poverty and ignorance and disease and inequality of opportunity. The ambition of the greatest man of our generation has been to wipe every tear from every eye. That may be beyond us, but as long as there are tears and suffering, so long our work will not be over.

And so we have to labour and to work, and work hard, to give reality to our dreams. Those dreams are for India, but they are also for the world, for all the nations and peoples are too closely knit together today for any one of them to imagine that it can live apart Peace has been said to be indivisible; so is freedom, so is prosperity now, and so also is disaster in this One World that can no longer be split into isolated fragments.

To the people of India, whose representatives we are, we make an appeal to join us with faith and confidence in this great adventure. This is no time for petty and destructive criticism, no time for ill-will or blaming others. We have to build the noble mansion of free India where all her children may dwell.

The appointed day has come–the day appointed by destiny–and India stands forth again, after long slumber and struggle, awake, vital, free and independent. The past clings on to us still in some measure and we have to do much before we redeem the pledges we have so often taken. Yet the turning-point is past, and history begins anew for us, the history which we shall live and act and others will write about.

It is a fateful moment for us in India, for all Asia and for the world. A new star rises, the star of freedom in the East, a new hope comes into being, a vision long cherished materializes. May the star never set and that hope never be betrayed!

We rejoice in that freedom, even though clouds surround us, and many of our people are sorrow-stricken and difficult problems encompass us. But freedom brings responsibilities and burdens and we have to face them in the spirit of a free and disciplined people.

On this day our first thoughts go to the architect of this freedom, the Father of our Nation [Gandhi], who, embodying the old spirit of India, held aloft the torch of freedom and lighted up the darkness that surrounded us. We have often been unworthy followers of his and have strayed from his message, but not only we but succeeding generations will remember this message and bear the imprint in their hearts of this great son of India, magnificent in his faith and strength and courage and humility. We shall never allow that torch of freedom to be blown out, however high the wind or stormy the tempest.

Our next thoughts must be of the unknown volunteers and soldiers of freedom who, without praise or reward, have served India even unto death.

We think also of our brothers and sisters who have been cut off from us by political boundaries and who unhappily cannot share at present in the freedom that has come. They are of us and will remain of us whatever may happen, and we shall be sharers in their good [or] ill fortune alike.

The future beckons to us. Whither do we go and what shall be our endeavour? To bring freedom and opportunity to the common man, to the peasants and workers of India; to fight and end poverty and ignorance and disease; to build up a prosperous, democratic and progressive nation, and to create social, economic and political institutions which will ensure justice and fullness of life to every man and woman.

We have hard work ahead. There is no resting for any one of us till we redeem our pledge in full, till we make all the people of India what destiny intended them to be. We are citizens of a great country on the verge of bold advance, and we have to live up to that high standard. All of us, to whatever religion we may belong, are equally the children of India with equal rights, privileges and obligations. We cannot encourage communalism or narrow-mindedness, for no nation can be great whose people are narrow in thought or in action.

To the nations and peoples of the world we send greetings and pledge ourselves to cooperate with them in furthering peace, freedom and democracy.

And to India, our much-loved motherland, the ancient, the eternal and the ever-new, we pay our reverent homage and we bind ourselves afresh to her service.

JAI HIND.

■

Biographical Sketch: John Fitzgerald Kennedy (May 29, 1917–November 22, 1963) was the 35th President of the United States. He served from 1961 until his assassination in 1963. He is also referred to as John F. Kennedy, JFK, John Kennedy or Jack Kennedy. Kennedy was a very fast reader.

He was also a master orator. In a speech given in December 1961, he set a record as the world's fastest public speaker by speaking 327 words in one minute.

Speeches By: John F. Kennedy

Topic: Address to the Greater Houston Ministerial Association

Date: September 12, 1960 at the Rice Hotel in Houston

Reverend Meza, Reverend Reck, I'm grateful for your generous invitation to state my views.

While the so-called religious issue is necessarily and properly the chief topic here tonight, I want to emphasize from the outset that I believe that we have far more critical issues in the 1960 campaign; the spread of Communist influence, until it now festers only 90 miles from the coast of Florida–the humiliating treatment of our President and Vice President by those who no longer respect our power–the hungry children I saw in West Virginia, the old people who cannot pay their doctors bills, the families forced to give up their farms–an America with too many slums, with too few schools, and too late to the moon and outer space. These are the real issues which should decide this campaign. And they are not religious issues–for war and hunger and ignorance and despair know no religious barrier.

But because I am a Catholic, and no Catholic has ever been elected President, the real issues in this campaign have been obscured–perhaps deliberately, in some quarters less responsible than this. So it is apparently necessary for me to state once again–not what kind of church I believe in, for that should be important only to me–but what kind of America I believe in.

I believe in an America where the separation of church and state is absolute; where no Catholic prelate would tell the President–should he be Catholic–how to act, and no Protestant minister would tell his parishioners for whom to vote; where no church or church school is granted any public funds or political preference, and where no man is denied public office merely because his religion differs from the President who might appoint him, or the people who might elect him.

I believe in an America that is officially neither Catholic, Protestant nor Jewish; where no public official either requests or accept instructions on public policy from the Pope, the National Council of Churches or any other ecclesiastical source; where no religious body seeks to impose its will directly or indirectly upon the general populace or the public acts of its officials, and where religious liberty is so indivisible that an act against one church is treated as an act against all.

For while this year it may be a Catholic against whom the finger of suspicion is pointed, in other years it has been–and may someday be again–a Jew, or a Quaker, or a Unitarian, or a Baptist. It was Virginia's harassment of Baptist preachers, for example, that led to Jefferson's statute of religious freedom. Today, I may be the victim, but tomorrow it may be you–until the whole fabric of our harmonious society is ripped apart at a time of great national peril.

Finally, I believe in an America where religious intolerance will someday end, where all men and all churches are treated as equals, where every man has the same right to attend or not to attend the church of his choice, where there is no Catholic vote, no anti-Catholic vote, no bloc voting of any kind, and where Catholics, Protestants, and Jews, at both the lay and the pastoral levels, will refrain from those attitudes of disdain and division which have so often marred their works in the past, and promote instead the American ideal of brotherhood.

That is the kind of America in which I believe. And it represents the kind of Presidency in which I believe, a great office that must be neither humbled by making it the instrument of any religious group nor tarnished by arbitrarily withholding it–its occupancy from the members of any one religious group. I believe in a President whose views on religion are his own private affair, neither imposed upon him by the nation, nor imposed by the nation upon him as a condition to holding that office.

I would not look with favor upon a President working to subvert the first amendment's guarantees of religious liberty; nor would our system of checks and balances permit him to do so. And neither do I look with favor upon those who would work to subvert Article VI of the Constitution by requiring a religious test, even by indirection. For if they disagree with that safeguard, they should be openly working to repeal it.

I want a Chief Executive whose public acts are responsible to all and obligated to none, who can attend any ceremony, service, or dinner his office may appropriately require of him to fulfill; and whose fulfillment of his Presidential office is not limited or conditioned by any religious oath, ritual, or obligation.

This is the kind of America I believe in–and this is the kind of America I fought for in the South Pacific, and the kind my brother died for in Europe. No one suggested then that we might have a divided loyalty, that we did not believe in liberty, or that we belonged to a disloyal group that threatened–I quote–"the freedoms for which our forefathers died."

And in fact this is the kind of America for which our forefathers did die when they fled here to escape religious test oaths that denied office to members of less favored churches–when they fought for the Constitution, the Bill of Rights, the Virginia Statute of Religious Freedom–and when they fought at the shrine I visited today, the Alamo. For side by side with Bowie and Crockett died Fuentes, and McCafferty, and Bailey, and Badillo, and Carey–but no one knows whether they were Catholics or not. For there was no religious test there.

I ask you tonight to follow in that tradition–to judge me on the basis of 14 years in the Congress, on my declared stands against an Ambassador to the Vatican, against unconstitutional aid to parochial schools, and against any boycott of the public schools–which I attended myself. And instead of doing this, do not judge me on the basis of these pamphlets and publications we all have seen that carefully select quotations out of context from the statements of Catholic church leaders, usually in other countries, frequently in other centuries, and rarely relevant to any situation here. And always omitting, of course, the statement of the American Bishops in 1948 which strongly endorsed Church-State separation, and which more nearly reflects the views of almost every American Catholic.

I do not consider these other quotations binding upon my public acts. Why should you?

But let me say, with respect to other countries, that I am wholly opposed to the State being used by any religious group, Catholic or Protestant, to compel, prohibit, or prosecute the free exercise of any other religion. And that goes for any persecution, at any time, by anyone, in any country. And I hope that you and I condemn with equal fervor those nations which deny their Presidency to Protestants, and those which deny it to Catholics. And rather than cite the misdeeds of those who differ, I would also cite the record of the Catholic Church in such nations as

France and Ireland, and the independence of such statesmen as De Gaulle and Adenauer.

But let me stress again that these are my views.

For contrary to common newspaper usage, I am not the Catholic candidate for President.

I am the Democratic Party's candidate for President who happens also to be a Catholic.

I do not speak for my church on public matters; and the church does not speak for me. Whatever issue may come before me as President, if I should be elected, on birth control, divorce, censorship, gambling or any other subject, I will make my decision in accordance with these views–in accordance with what my conscience tells me to be in the national interest, and without regard to outside religious pressure or dictates. And no power or threat of punishment could cause me to decide otherwise.

But if the time should ever come–and I do not concede any conflict to be remotely possible–when my office would require me to either violate my conscience or violate the national interest, then I would resign the office; and I hope any conscientious public servant would do likewise.

But I do not intend to apologize for these views to my critics of either Catholic or Protestant faith; nor do I intend to disavow either my views or my church in order to win this election.

If I should lose on the real issues, I shall return to my seat in the Senate, satisfied that I'd tried my best and was fairly judged.

But if this election is decided on the basis that 40 million Americans lost their chance of being President on the day they were baptized, then it is the whole nation that will be the loser, in the eyes of Catholics and non-Catholics around the world, in the eyes of history, and in the eyes of our own people.

But if, on the other hand, I should win this election, then I shall devote every effort of mind and spirit to fulfilling the oath of the Presidency–practically identical, I might add, with the oath I have taken for 14 years in the Congress. For without reservation, I can, "Solemnly swear that I will faithfully execute the office of President of the United States, and will to the best of my ability preserve, protect, and defend the Constitution–so help me God."

★

Second Speech by: John F. Kennedy

Topic: Man on the Moon

Date: May 25, 1961

Mr. Speaker, Mr. Vice President, my co-partners in Government, gentlemen and ladies:

The Constitution imposes upon me the obligation to "from time to time give to the Congress information of the State of the Union." While this has traditionally been interpreted as an annual affair, this tradition has been broken in extraordinary times.

These are extraordinary times. And we face an extraordinary challenge. Our strength as well as our convictions have imposed upon this nation the role of leader in freedom's cause. No role in history could be more difficult or more important. We stand for freedom. That is our conviction for ourselves-that is our only commitment to others. No friend, no neutral and no adversary should think otherwise. We are not against any man-or any nation-or any system-except as it is hostile to freedom. Nor am I here to present a new military doctrine, bearing any one name or aimed at any one area. I am here to promote the freedom doctrine. ...

IX. Space

Finally, if we are to win the battle that is now going on around the world between freedom and tyranny, the dramatic achievements in space which occurred in recent weeks should have made clear to us all, as did the Sputnik in 1957, the impact of this adventure on the minds of men everywhere, who are attempting to make a determination of which road they should take. Since early in my term, our efforts in space have been under review. With the advice of the Vice President, who is Chairman of the National Space Council, we have examined where we are strong and where we are not, where we may succeed and where we may not. Now it is time to take longer strides-time for a great new American enterprise-time for this nation to take a clearly leading role in space achievement, which in many ways may hold the key to our future on earth.

I believe we possess all the resources and talents necessary. But the facts of the matter are that we have never made the national decisions or marshaled the national resources required for such leadership. We have never specified long-range goals on an urgent time schedule, or managed our resources and our time so as to insure their fulfillment.

Recognizing the head start obtained by the Soviets with their large rocket engines, which gives them many months of lead-time, and recognizing the likelihood that they will exploit this lead for some time to come in still more impressive successes, we nevertheless are required to make new efforts on our own. For while we cannot guarantee that we shall one day be first, we can guarantee that any failure to make this effort will make us last. We take an additional risk by making it in full view of the world, but as shown by the feat of astronaut Shepard, this very risk enhances our stature when we are successful. But this is not merely a race. Space is open to us now; and our eagerness to share its meaning is not governed by the efforts of others. We go into space because whatever mankind must undertake, free men must fully share.

I therefore ask the Congress, above and beyond the increases I have earlier requested for space activities, to provide the funds which are needed to meet the following national goals:

First, I believe that this nation should commit itself to achieving the goal, before this decade is out, of landing a man on the moon and returning him safely to the earth. No single space project in this period will be more impressive to mankind, or more important for the long-range exploration of space; and none will be so difficult or expensive to accomplish. We propose to accelerate the development of the appropriate lunar space craft. We propose to develop alternate liquid and solid fuel boosters, much larger than any now being developed, until certain which is superior.

We propose additional funds for other engine development and for unmanned explorations–explorations which are particularly important for one purpose which this nation will never overlook: the survival of the man who first makes this daring flight. But in a very real sense, it will not be one man going to the moon-if we make this judgment affirmatively, it will be an entire nation. For all of us must work to put him there.

Secondly, an additional 23 million dollars, together with 7 million dollars already available, will accelerate development of the Rover nuclear rocket. This gives promise of some day providing a means for even more exciting and ambitious exploration of space, perhaps beyond the moon, perhaps to the very end of the solar system itself.

Third, an additional 50 million dollars will make the most of our present leadership, by accelerating the use of space satellites for world-wide communications. Fourth, an additional 75 million dollars-of which 53 million dollars is for the Weather Bureau-will help give us at the earliest possible time a satellite system for world-wide weather observation.

Let it be clear-and this is a judgment which the Members of the Congress must finally make-let if be clear that I am asking the Congress and the country to accept a firm commitment to a new course of action-a course which will last for many years and carry very heavy costs: 531 million dollars in fiscal '62–an estimated seven to nine billion dollars additional over the next five years. If we are to go only half way, or reduce our sights in the face of difficulty, in my judgment it would be better not to go at all.

Now this is a choice which this country must make, and I am confident that under the leadership of the Space Committees of the Congress, and the Appropriating Committees, that you will consider the matter carefully.

It is a most important decision that we make as a nation. But all of you have lived through the last four years and have seen the significance of space and the adventures in space, and no one can predict with certainty what the ultimate meaning will be of mastery of space. I believe we should go to the moon. But I think every citizen of this country as well as the Members of the Congress should consider the matter carefully in making their judgment, to which we have given attention over many weeks and months, because it is a heavy burden, and there is no sense in agreeing or desiring that the United States take an affirmative position in outer space, unless we are prepared to do the work and bear the burdens to make it successful. If we are not, we should decide today and this year. This decision demands a major national commitment of scientific and technical manpower, materiel and facilities, and the possibility of their diversion from other important activities where they are already thinly spread. It means a degree of dedication, organization and discipline which have not always characterized our research and development efforts. It means we cannot afford undue work stoppages, inflated costs of material or talent, wasteful interagency rivalries, or a high turnover of key personnel.

New objectives and new money cannot solve these problems. They could in fact, aggravate them further-unless every scientist, every engineer, every serviceman, every technician, contractor, and civil servant gives his personal pledge that this nation will move forward, with the full speed of freedom, in the exciting adventure of space.

■

Biographical Sketch: Jonathan Edwards (October 5, 1703–March 22, 1758) was a colonial American Congregational preacher and theologian. He is popular as one of the greatest and most profound of American theologians and revivalists. His is often associated with his defense of Calvinist theology and the Puritan heritage. His fire-and-brimstone sermons, such as 'Sinners in the hands of an angry God,' emphasised the unworthiness of man in God's eyes.

Speech By: Jonathan Edwards

Topic: Sinners in the Hands of an Angry God

Date: July 8, 1741

–Their foot shall slide in due time.–Deuteronomy 32:35

In this verse is threatened the vengeance of God on the wicked unbelieving Israelites, who were God's visible people, and who lived under the means of grace; but who, notwithstanding all God's wonderful works towards them, remained (as verse 28.) void of counsel, having no understanding in them. Under all the cultivations of heaven, they brought forth bitter and poisonous fruit; as in the two verses next preceding the text.–The expression I have chosen for my text, **their foot shall slide in due time**, seems to imply the following things, relating to the punishment and destruction to which these wicked Israelites were exposed.

1. That they were always exposed to **destruction**; as one that stands or walks in slippery places is always exposed to fall.

This is implied in the manner of their destruction coming upon them, being represented by their foot sliding. The same is expressed, Psalm 72:18. "*Surely thou didst set them in slippery places; thou castedst them down into destruction.*"

2. It implies that they were always exposed to **sudden unexpected** destruction. As he that walks in slippery places is every moment liable to fall, he cannot foresee one moment whether he shall stand or fall the next; and when he does fall, he falls at once without warning: Which is also expressed in Psalm 73:18,19. "*Surely thou didst set them in slippery places; thou castedst them down into destruction: How are they brought into desolation as in a moment!*"
3. Another thing implied is, that they are liable to fall **of themselves**, without being thrown down by the hand of another; as he that stands or walks on slippery ground needs nothing but his own weight to throw him down.
4. That the reason why they are not fallen already and do not fall now is only that God's appointed time is not come. For it is said, that when that due time, or appointed time comes, **their foot shall slide**. Then they shall be left to fall, as they are inclined by their own weight. God will not hold them up in these slippery places any longer, but will let them go; and then, at that very instant, they shall fall into destruction; as he that stands on such slippery declining ground, on the edge of a pit, he cannot stand alone, when he is let go he immediately falls and is lost.

The observation from the words that I would now insist upon is this.–"There is nothing that keeps wicked men at any one moment out of hell, but the mere pleasure of God."–By the **mere** pleasure of God, I mean his **sovereign** pleasure, his arbitrary will, restrained by no obligation, hindered by no manner of difficulty, any more than if nothing else but God's mere will had in the least degree, or in any respect whatsoever, any hand in the preservation of wicked men one moment.–The truth of this observation may appear by the following considerations.

1. There is no want of **power** in God to cast wicked men into hell at any moment. Men's hands cannot be strong when God rises up. The strongest have no power to resist him, nor can any deliver out of his hands.–He is not only able to cast wicked men into hell, but he can most easily do it. Sometimes an earthly prince meets with a great deal of difficulty to subdue a rebel, who has found means to fortify himself, and has made himself strong by the numbers of his followers. But it is not so with God. There is no fortress that is any defence from the power of God. Though hand joins in hand, and vast multitudes of God's enemies combine and associate themselves, they are easily broken in pieces. They are as great heaps of light chaff before the whirlwind; or large quantities of dry stubble before devouring flames. We find it easy to tread on and crush a worm that we see crawling on the earth; so it is easy for us to cut or singe a slender thread that any thing hangs by: thus easy is it for God, when he pleases, to cast his enemies down to hell. What are we that we should think to stand before him, at whose rebuke the earth trembles, and before whom the rocks are thrown down?

2. They **deserve** to be cast into hell; so that divine justice never stands in the way, it makes no objection against God's using his power at any moment to destroy them. Yea, on the contrary, justice calls aloud for an infinite punishment of their sins. Divine justice says of the tree that brings forth such grapes of Sodom, "*Cut it down, why cumbereth it the ground?*" Luke 13:7. The sword of divine justice is every moment brandished over their heads, and it is nothing but the hand of arbitrary mercy, and God's mere will, that holds it back.

3. They are already under a sentence of **condemnation** to hell. They do not only justly deserve to be cast down thither, but the sentence of the law of God, that eternal and immutable rule of righteousness that God has fixed between him and mankind, is gone out against them, and stands against them; so that they are bound over already to hell. John 3:18. "*He that believeth not is condemned already.*" So that every unconverted man properly belongs to hell; that is his place; from thence he is, John 8:23. "*Ye are from beneath:*" And thither he is bound; it is the place that justice, and God's word, and the sentence of his unchangeable law assign to him.

4. They are now the objects of that very same **anger** and wrath of God that is expressed in the torments of hell. And the reason why they do not go down to hell at each moment, is not because God, in whose power they are, is not then very angry with them; as he is with many miserable creatures now tormented in hell, who there feel and bear the fierceness of his wrath. Yea, God is a great deal more angry with great numbers that are now on earth: yea, doubtless, with many that are now in this congregation, who it may be are at ease, than he is with many of those who are now in the flames of hell.

   So that it is not because God is unmindful of their wickedness, and does not resent it, that he does not let loose his hand and cut them off. God is not altogether such one as themselves, though they may imagine him to be so. The wrath of God bums against them, their damnation does not slumber; the pit is prepared, the fire is made ready, the furnace is now hot, ready to receive them; the flames do now rage and glow. The glittering sword is whet, and held over them, and the pit hath opened its mouth under them.

5. The devil stands ready to fall upon them, and seize them as his own, at what moment God shall permit him. They belong to him; he has their souls in his possession, and under his dominion. The scripture represents them as his goods, Luke 11:12. The devils watch them; they are ever by them at their right hand; they stand waiting for them, like greedy hungry lions that see their prey, and expect to have it, but are for the present kept back. If God should withdraw his hand, by which they are restrained, they would in one moment fly upon their poor souls. The old serpent is gaping for them; hell opens its mouth wide to receive them; and if God should permit it, they would be hastily swallowed up and lost.

6. There are in the souls of wicked men those hellish principles reigning, that would presently kindle and flame out into hell fire, if it were not for God's restraints. There is laid in the very nature of carnal men, a foundation for the torments of hell. There are those corrupt principles, in reigning power in them, and in full possession of them, that are seeds of hell fire. These principles are active and powerful, exceeding violent in their nature, and if it were not for the restraining hand of God upon them, they would soon break out, they would flame out after the same manner as the same corruptions, the same enmity does in the hearts of damned souls, and would beget the same torments as they do in them. The souls of the wicked are in scripture compared to the troubled sea, Isa. 57:20. For the present, God restrains their wickedness by his mighty power, as he does the raging waves of the troubled sea, saying, "*Hitherto shalt thou come, but no further;*" but if God should withdraw that restraining power, it would soon carry all before it. Sin is the ruin and misery of the soul; it is destructive in its nature; and if God should leave it without restraint, there would need nothing else to make the soul perfectly miserable. The corruption

of the heart of man is immoderate and boundless in its fury; and while wicked me live here, it is like fire pent up by God's restraints, whereas if it were let loose, it would set on fire the course of nature; and as the heart is now a sink of sin, so if sin was not restrained, it would immediately turn the soul into fiery oven, or a furnace of fire and brimstone.

7. It is no security to wicked men for one moment, that there are no visible means of death at hand. It is no security to a natural man, that he is now in health, and that he does not see which way he should now immediately go out of the world by any accident, and that there is no visible danger in any respect in his circumstances. The manifold and continual experience of the world in all ages, shows this is no evidence, that a man is not on the very brink of eternity, and that the next step will not be into another world. The unseen, unthought-of ways and means of persons going suddenly out of the world are innumerable and inconceivable. Unconverted men walk over the pit of hell on a rotten covering, and there are innumerable places in this covering so weak that they will not bear their weight, and these places are not seen. The arrows of death fly unseen at noon-day; the sharpest sight cannot discern them. God has so many different unsearchable ways of taking wicked men out of the world and sending them to hell, that there is nothing to make it appear, that God had need to be at the expense of a miracle, or go out of the ordinary course of his providence, to destroy any wicked man, at any moment. All the means that there are of sinners going out of the world, are so in God's hands, and so universally and absolutely subject to his power and determination, that it does not depend at all the less on the mere will of God, whether sinners shall at any moment go to hell, than if means were never made use of, or at all concerned in the case.

8. Natural men's prudence and care to preserve their own lives, or the care of others to preserve them, do not secure them a moment. To this, divine providence and universal experience do also bear testimony. There is this clear evidence that men's own wisdom is no security to them from death; that if it were otherwise we should see some difference between the wise and politic men of the world, and others, with regard to their liableness to early and unexpected death: but how is it in fact? Eccles. 2:16. "*How dieth the wise man? even as the fool.*"

9. All wicked men's pains and **contrivance** which they use to escape hell, while they continue to reject Christ, and so remain wicked men, do not secure them from hell one moment. Almost every natural man that hears of hell, flatters himself that he shall escape it; he depends upon himself for his own security; he flatters himself in what he has done, in what he is now doing, or what he intends to do. Every one lays out matters in his own mind how he shall avoid damnation, and flatters himself that he contrives well for himself, and that his schemes will not fail. They hear indeed that there are but few saved, and that the greater part of men that have died heretofore are gone to hell; but each one imagines that he lays out matters better for his own escape than others have done. He does not intend to come to that place of torment; he says within himself, that he intends to take effectual care, and to order matters so for himself as not to fail.

But the foolish children of men miserably delude themselves in their own schemes, and in confidence in their own strength and wisdom; they trust to nothing but a shadow. The greater part of those who heretofore have lived under the same means of grace, and are now dead, are undoubtedly gone to hell; and it was not because they were not as wise as those who are now alive: it was not because they did not lay out matters as well for themselves to secure their own escape. If we could speak with them, and inquire of them, one by one, whether they expected, when alive, and when they used to hear about hell, ever to be the subjects of misery: we doubtless, should hear one and another reply, "No, I never intended to come here: I had laid out matters otherwise in my mind; I thought I should contrive well for myself–I thought my scheme good. I intended to take effectual care; but it came upon me unexpected; I did not look for it at that time, and in that manner; it came as a thief–Death outwitted me: God's wrath was too quick for me. Oh, my cursed foolishness! I was flattering myself, and pleasing myself with vain dreams of what I would do hereafter; and when I was saying, Peace and safety, then sudden destruction came upon me."

10. God has laid himself under no **obligation**, by any promise to keep any natural man out of hell one moment. God certainly has made no promises either of eternal life, or of any deliverance or preservation from eternal death, but what are contained in the covenant of grace, the promises that are given in Christ, in whom all the promises are yea and amen. But surely they have no interest in the promises of the covenant of grace who are not the children of the covenant, who do not believe in any of the promises, and have no interest in the Mediator of the covenant.

So that, whatever some have imagined and pretended about promises made to natural men's earnest seeking and knocking, it is plain and manifest, that whatever pains a natural man takes in religion, whatever prayers he makes, till he believes in Christ, God is under no manner of obligation to keep him a moment from eternal destruction.

So that, thus it is that natural men are held in the hand of God, over the pit of hell; they have deserved the fiery pit, and are already sentenced to it; and God is dreadfully provoked, his anger is as great towards them as to those that are actually suffering the executions of the fierceness of his wrath in hell, and they have done nothing in the least to appease or abate that anger, neither is God in the least bound by any promise to hold them up one moment; the devil is waiting for them, hell is gaping for them, the flames gather and flash about them, and would fain lay hold on them, and swallow them up; the fire pent up in their own hearts is struggling to break out: and they have no interest in any Mediator, there are no means within reach that can be any security to them. In short, they have no refuge, nothing to take hold of; all that preserves them every moment is the mere arbitrary will, and uncovenanted, unobliged forbearance of an incensed God.

Application

The use of this awful subject may be for awakening unconverted persons in this congregation. This that you have heard is the case of every one of you that are out of Christ.–That world of misery, that take of burning brimstone, is extended abroad under you. There is the dreadful pit of the glowing flames of the wrath of God; there is hell's wide gaping mouth open; and you have nothing to stand upon, nor any thing to take hold of; there is nothing between you and hell but the air; it is only the power and mere pleasure of God that holds you up.

You probably are not sensible of this; you find you are kept out of hell, but do not see the hand of God in it; but look at other things, as the good state of your bodily constitution, your care of your own life, and the means you use for your own preservation. But indeed these things are nothing; if God should withdraw his hand, they would avail no more to keep you from falling, than the thin air to hold up a person that is suspended in it.

Your wickedness makes you as it were heavy as lead, and to tend downwards with great weight and pressure towards hell; and if God should let you go, you would immediately sink and swiftly descend and plunge into the bottomless gulf, and your healthy constitution, and your own care and prudence, and best contrivance, and all your righteousness, would have no more influence to uphold you and keep you out of hell, than a spider's web would have to stop a falling rock. Were it not for the sovereign pleasure of God, the earth would not bear you one moment; for you are a burden to it; the creation groans with you; the creature is made subject to the bondage of your corruption, not willingly; the sun does not willingly shine upon you to give you light to serve sin and Satan; the earth does not willingly yield her increase to satisfy your lusts; nor is it willingly a stage for your wickedness to be acted upon; the air does not willingly serve you for breath to maintain the flame of life in your vitals, while you spend your life in the service of God's enemies. God's creatures are good, and were made for men to serve God with, and do not willingly subserve to any other purpose, and groan when they are abused to purposes so directly contrary to their nature and end. And the world would spew you out, were it not for the sovereign hand of him who hath subjected it in hope. There are the black clouds of God's wrath now hanging directly over your heads, full of the dreadful storm, and big with thunder; and were it not for the restraining hand of God, it would immediately burst forth upon you. The sovereign pleasure of God, for the present, stays his rough wind; otherwise it would come with fury, and your destruction would come like a whirlwind, and you would be like the chaff of the summer threshing floor.

The wrath of God is like great waters that are dammed for the present; they increase more and more, and rise higher and higher, till an outlet is given; and the longer the stream is stopped, the more rapid and mighty is its course, when once it is let loose. It is true, that judgment against your evil works has not been executed hitherto; the floods of God's vengeance have been withheld; but your guilt in the mean time is constantly increasing, and you are every day treasuring up more wrath; the waters are constantly rising, and waxing more and more mighty; and there is nothing but the mere pleasure of God, that holds the waters back, that are unwilling to be stopped, and press hard to go forward. If God should only withdraw his hand from the flood-gate, it would immediately fly open, and the fiery floods of the fierceness and wrath of God, would rush forth with inconceivable fury, and would come upon you with omnipotent power; and if your strength were ten thousand times greater than it is, yea, ten thousand times greater than the strength of the stoutest, sturdiest devil in hell, it would be nothing to withstand or endure it.

The bow of God's wrath is bent, and the arrow made ready on the string, and justice bends the arrow at your heart, and strains the bow, and it is nothing but the mere pleasure of God, and that of an angry God, without any promise or obligation at all, that keeps the arrow one moment from being made drunk with your blood. Thus all you that never passed under a great change of heart, by the mighty power of the Spirit of God upon your souls; all you that were never born again, and made new creatures, and raised from being dead in sin, to a state of new, and before altogether unexperienced light and life, are in the hands of an angry God. However you may have reformed your life in many things, and may have had religious affections, and may keep up a form of religion in your families and closets, and in the house of God, it is nothing but his mere pleasure that keeps you from being this moment swallowed up in everlasting destruction. However unconvinced you may now be of the truth of what you hear, by and by you will be fully convinced of it. Those that are gone from being in the like circumstances with you, see that it was so with them; for destruction came suddenly upon most of them; when they expected nothing of it, and while they were saying, Peace and safety: now they see, that those things on which they depended for peace and safety, were nothing but thin air and empty shadows.

The God that holds you over the pit of hell, much as one holds a spider, or some loathsome insect over the fire, abhors you, and is dreadfully provoked: his wrath towards you burns like fire; he looks upon you as worthy of nothing else, but to be cast into the fire; he is of purer eyes than to bear to have you in his sight; you are ten thousand times more abominable in his eyes, than the most hateful venomous serpent is in ours. You have offended him infinitely more than ever a stubborn rebel did his prince; and yet it is nothing but his hand that holds you from falling into the fire every moment. It is to be ascribed to nothing else, that you did not go to hell the last night; that you was suffered to awake again in this world, after you closed your eyes to sleep. And there is no other reason to be given, why you have not dropped into hell since you arose in the morning, but that God's hand has held you up. There is no other reason to be given why you have not gone to hell, since you have sat here in the house of God, provoking his pure eyes by your sinful wicked manner of attending his solemn worship. Yea, there is nothing else that is to be given as a reason why you do not this very moment drop down into hell.

O sinner! Consider the fearful danger you are in: it is a great furnace of wrath, a wide and bottomless pit, full of the fire of wrath, that you are held over in the hand of that God, whose wrath is provoked and incensed as much against you, as against many of the damned in hell. You hang by a slender thread, with the flames of divine wrath flashing about it, and ready every moment to singe it, and burn it asunder; and you have no interest in any Mediator, and nothing to lay hold of to save yourself, nothing to keep off the flames of wrath, nothing of your own, nothing that you ever have done, nothing that you can do, to induce God to spare you one moment.–And consider here more particularly;

1. **Whose** wrath it is: it is the wrath of the infinite God. If it were only the wrath of man, though it were of the most potent prince, it would be comparatively little to be regarded. The wrath of kings is very much dreaded, especially of absolute monarchs, who have the possessions and lives of their subjects wholly in their power, to be disposed of at their mere will. Prov. 20:2. "*The fear of a king is as the roaring of a lion: Whoso provoketh him to anger, sinneth against his own soul.*" The subject that very much enrages an arbitrary prince, is liable to suffer the most extreme torments that human art can invent, or human power can inflict. But the greatest earthly potentates in their greatest majesty and strength, and when clothed in their greatest terrors, are but feeble, despicable worms of the dust, in comparison of the great and almighty Creator and King of heaven and earth. It is but little that they can do, when most enraged, and when they have exerted the utmost of their fury. All the kings of the earth, before God are as grasshoppers; they are nothing, and less than nothing: both their love and their hatred is to be despised. The wrath of the great King of kings, is as much more terrible than theirs, as his majesty is greater. Luke 12:4,5. "*And I say unto you, my friends, Be not afraid of them that kill the body, and after that, have no more that they can do. But I will forewarn you whom you shall fear: fear him, which after he hath killed, hath power to cast into hell: yea, I say unto you, Fear him.*"

2. It is the **fierceness** of his wrath that you are exposed to. We often read of the fury of God; as in Isa. 59:18. "*According to their deeds, accordingly he will repay fury to his adversaries.*" So Isa. 66:15. "*For behold, the Lord will come with fire, and with his chariots like a whirlwind, to render his anger with fury, and his rebuke with flames of fire.*" And in many other places. So, Rev. 19:15, we read of "*the wine press of the*

fierceness and wrath of Almighty God." The words are exceeding terrible. If it had only been said, "*the wrath of God,*" the words would have implied that which is infinitely dreadful: but it is "*the fierceness and wrath of God.*" The fury of God! the fierceness of Jehovah! Oh, how dreadful that must be! Who can utter or conceive what such expressions carry in them! But it is also "*the fierceness and wrath of almighty God.*" As though there would be a very great manifestation of his almighty power in what the fierceness of his wrath should inflict, as though omnipotence should be as it were enraged, and exerted, as men are wont to exert their strength in the fierceness of their wrath. Oh! then, what will be the consequence! What will become of the poor worms that shall suffer it! Whose hands can be strong? And whose heart can endure? To what a dreadful, inexpressible, inconceivable depth of misery must the poor creature be sunk who shall be the subject of this!

Consider this, you that are here present, that yet remain in an unregenerate state. That God will execute the fierceness of his anger, implies, that he will inflict wrath without any pity. When God beholds the ineffable extremity of your case, and sees your torment to be so fastly disproportioned to your strength, and sees how your poor soul is crushed, and sinks down, as it were, into an infinite gloom; he will have no compassion upon you, he will not forbear the executions of his wrath, or in the least lighten his hand; there shall be no moderation or mercy, nor will God then at all stay his rough wind; he will have no regard to your welfare, nor be at all careful lest you should suffer too much in any other sense, than only that you shall **not suffer beyond what strict justice requires**. Nothing shall be withheld, because it is so hard for you to bear. Ezek. 8:18. "*Therefore will I also deal in fury: mine eye shall not spare, neither will I have pity; and though they cry in mine ears with* *a loud voice, yet I will not hear them.*" Now God stands ready to pity you; this is a day of mercy; you may cry now with some encouragement of obtaining mercy. But when once the day of mercy is past, your most lamentable and dolorous cries and shrieks will be in vain; you will be wholly lost and thrown away of God, as to any regard to your welfare. God will have no other use to put you to, but to suffer misery; you shall be continued in being to no other end; for you will be a vessel of wrath fitted to destruction; and there will be no other use of this vessel, but to be filled full of wrath. God will be so far from pitying you when you cry to him, that it is said he will only "*laugh and mock,*" Prov. 1:25, 26, & c.

How awful are those words, Isa. 63:3, which are the words of the great God. "*I will tread them in mine anger, and will trample them in my fury, and their blood shall be sprinkled upon my garments, and I will stain all my raiment.*" It is perhaps impossible to conceive of words that carry in them greater manifestations of these three things, viz. contempt, and hatred, and fierceness of indignation. If you cry to God to pity you, he will be so far from pitying you in your doleful case, or showing you the least regard or favour, that instead of that, he will only tread you under foot. And though he will know that you cannot bear the weight of omnipotence treading upon you, yet he will not regard that, but he will crush you under his feet without mercy; he will crush out your blood, and make it fly, and it shall be sprinkled on his garments, so as to stain all his raiment. He will not only hate you, but he will have you in the utmost contempt: no place shall be thought fit for you, but under his feet to be trodden down as the mire of the streets.

3. The **misery** you are exposed to is that which God will inflict to that end, that he might show what that wrath of Jehovah is. God hath had it on his heart to show to angels and men,

both how excellent his love is, and also how terrible his wrath is. Sometimes earthly kings have a mind to show how terrible their wrath is, by the extreme punishments they would execute on those that would provoke them. Nebuchadnezzar, that mighty and haughty monarch of the Chaldean empire, was willing to show his wrath when enraged with Shadrach, Meshach, and Abednego; and accordingly gave orders that the burning fiery furnace should be heated seven times hotter than it was before; doubtless, it was raised to the utmost degree of fierceness that human art could raise it. But the great God is also willing to show his wrath, and magnify his awful majesty and mighty power in the extreme sufferings of his enemies. Rom. 9:22. "*What if God, willing to show his wrath, and to make his power known, endured with much long-suffering the vessels of wrath fitted to destruction?*" And seeing this is his design, and what he has determined, even to show how terrible the unrestrained wrath, the fury and fierceness of Jehovah is, he will do it to effect. There will be something accomplished and brought to pass that will be dreadful with a witness. When the great and angry God hath risen up and executed his awful vengeance on the poor sinner, and the wretch is actually suffering the infinite weight and power of his indignation, then will God call upon the whole universe to behold that awful majesty and mighty power that is to be seen in it. Isa. 33:12-14. "*And the people shall be as the burnings of lime, as thorns cut up shall they be burnt in the fire. Hear ye that are far off, what I have done; and ye that are near, acknowledge my might. The sinners in Zion are afraid; fearfulness hath surprised the hypocrites,* " & c.

Thus it will be with you that are in an unconverted state, if you continue in it; the infinite might, and majesty, and terribleness of the omnipotent God shall be magnified upon you, in the ineffable strength of your torments. You shall be tormented in the presence of the holy angels, and in the presence of the Lamb; and when you shall be in this state of suffering, the glorious inhabitants of heaven shall go forth and look on the awful spectacle, that they may see what the wrath and fierceness of the Almighty is; and when they have seen it, they will fall down and adore that great power and majesty. Isa. 66:23,24. "*And it shall come to pass, that from one new moon to another, and from one sabbath to another, shall all flesh come to worship before me, saith the Lord. And they shall go forth and look upon the carcasses of the men that have transgressed against me; for their worm shall not die, neither shall their fire be quenched, and they shall be an abhorring unto all flesh.*"

4. It is **everlasting** wrath. It would be dreadful to suffer this fierceness and wrath of Almighty God one moment; but you must suffer it to all eternity. There will be no end to this exquisite horrible misery. When you look forward, you shall see a long for ever, a boundless duration before you, which will swallow up your thoughts, and amaze your soul; and you will absolutely despair of ever having any deliverance, any end, any mitigation, any rest at all. You will know certainly that you must wear out long ages, millions of millions of ages, in wrestling and conflicting with this almighty merciless vengeance; and then when you have so done, when so many ages have actually been spent by you in this manner, you will know that all is but a point to what remains. So that your punishment will indeed be infinite. Oh, who can express what the state of a soul in such circumstances is! All that we can possibly say about it, gives but a very feeble, faint representation of it; it is inexpressible and inconceivable: For "*who knows the power of God's anger?*"

How dreadful is the state of those that are daily and hourly in the danger of this great wrath and infinite misery! But this is the dismal case of every soul in this congregation that has not been born again, however moral and strict, sober and religious, they may otherwise be. Oh that you would consider it, whether you be young or old! There is reason to think that there are many in this congregation now hearing this discourse, that will actually be the subjects of this very misery to all eternity. We know not who they are, or in what seats they sit, or what thoughts they now have. It may be they are now at ease, and hear all these things without much disturbance, and are now flattering themselves that they are not the persons, promising themselves that they shall escape. If we knew that there was one person, and but one, in the whole congregation, that was to be the subject of this misery, what an awful thing would it be to think of! If we knew who it was, what an awful sight would it be to see such a person! How might all the rest of the congregation lift up a lamentable and bitter cry over him! But, alas! Instead of one, how many is it likely will remember this discourse in hell? And it would be a wonder, if some that are now present should not be in hell in a very short time, even before this year is out. And it would be no wonder if some persons, that now sit here, in some seats of this meeting-house, in health, quiet and secure, should be there before tomorrow morning. Those of you that finally continue in a natural condition that shall keep out of hell longest will be there in a little time! Your damnation does not slumber; it will come swiftly, and, in all probability, very suddenly upon many of you. You have reason to wonder that you are not already in hell. It is doubtless the case of some whom you have seen and known, that never deserved hell more than you, and that heretofore appeared as likely to have been now alive as you. Their case is past all hope; they are crying in extreme misery and perfect despair; but here you are in the land of the living and in the house of God, and have an opportunity to obtain salvation. What would not those poor damned hopeless souls give for one day's opportunity such as you now enjoy!

And now you have an extraordinary opportunity, a day wherein Christ has thrown the door of mercy wide open, and stands in calling and crying with a loud voice to poor sinners; a day wherein many are flocking to him, and pressing into the kingdom of God. Many are daily coming from the east, west, north and south; many that were very lately in the same miserable condition that you are in, are now in a happy state, with their hearts filled with love to him who has loved them, and washed them from their sins in his own blood, and rejoicing in hope of the glory of God. How awful is it to be left behind at such a day! To see so many others feasting, while you are pining and perishing! To see so many rejoicing and singing for joy of heart, while you have cause to mourn for sorrow of heart, and howl for vexation of spirit! How can you rest one moment in such a condition? Are not your souls as precious as the souls of the people at Suffield, where they are flocking from day to day to Christ?

Are there not many here who have lived long in the world, and are not to this day born again? And so are aliens from the commonwealth of Israel, and have done nothing ever since they have lived, but treasure up wrath against the day of wrath? Oh, sirs, your case, in an especial manner, is extremely dangerous. Your guilt and hardness of heart is extremely great. Do you not see how generaity persons of your years are passed over and left, in the present remarkable and wonderful dispensation of God's mercy? You had need to consider yourselves, and awake thoroughly out of sleep. You cannot bear the fierceness and wrath of the infinite God.–And you, young men, and young women, will you neglect this precious season which you now enjoy, when so many others of your age are renouncing all youthful vanities, and flocking to Christ? You especially have now an extraordinary opportunity; but if you neglect it, it will soon be with you as with those persons who spent all the precious days of youth in sin, and are now come to such a dreadful pass in blindness and hardness.–And you, children, who are unconverted, do not you know that you are going down to hell, to bear the dreadful wrath of that God, who is now angry with you every day and every night? Will you be content to be the children of the devil, when so many other children in the land are converted, and are become the holy and happy children of the King of kings?

And let every one that is yet out of Christ, and hanging over the pit of hell, whether they be old men and women, or middle aged, or young people, or little children, now hearken to the loud calls of God's word and providence. This acceptable year of the Lord, a day of such great favour to some, will doubtless be a day of as remarkable vengeance to others. Men's hearts harden, and their guilt increases apace at such a day as this, if they neglect their souls; and never was there so great danger of such persons being given up to hardness of heart and blindness of mind. God seems now to be hastily gathering in his elect in all parts of the land; and probably the greater part of adult persons that ever shall be saved, will be brought in now in a little time, and that it will be as it was on the great out-pouring of the Spirit upon the Jews in the apostles' days; the election will obtain, and the rest will be blinded. If this should be the case with you, you will eternally curse this day, and will curse the day that ever you was born, to see such a season of the pouring out of God's Spirit, and will wish that you had died and gone to hell before you had seen it. Now undoubtedly it is, as it was in the days of John the Baptist, the axe is in an extraordinary manner laid at the root of the trees, that every tree which brings not forth good fruit, may be hewn down and cast into the fire.

Therefore, let every one that is out of Christ, now awake and fly from the wrath to come. The wrath of Almighty God is now undoubtedly hanging over a great part of this congregation. Let every one fly out of Sodom: "Haste and escape for your lives, look not behind you, escape to the mountain, lest you be consumed."

■

Biographical Sketch: Kofi Atta Annan (born April 8, 1938) is a Ghanaian born diplomat. He served as the seventh Secretary-General of the United Nations from January 1, 1997 to December 31, 2006. He was succeeded by Ban Ki-moon. As Secretary-General, Mr. Annan gave priority to revitalising the UN through a comprehensive programme of reform; strengthening the organisation's traditional work in areas of development and maintenance of international peace and security. He advocated human rights, the rule of law and the universal values of equality, tolerance and human dignity.

Speeches By: Kofi A. Annan

Topic: Farewell statement to the General Assembly

Date: September 19, 2006

Madam President,

Excellencies,

Ladies and Gentlemen,

When I first spoke to you from this podium, in 1997, it seemed to me that humanity faced three great challenges.

One was to ensure that globalization would benefit the human race as a whole, not only its more fortunate members.

Another was to heal the disorder of the post-cold-war world, replacing it with a genuinely new world order of peace and freedom, as envisaged in our Charter.

And the third was to protect the rights and dignity of individuals, particularly women, which were so widely trampled underfoot.

As the second African to serve as Secretary-General, I felt that all three of these challenges–the security challenge; the development challenge; the challenge of human rights and the rule of law–concerned me directly.

Africa was in great danger of being excluded from the benefits of globalization–indeed, of being left to rot on the margins of the world economy.

Africa was also the scene of some of the most protracted and brutal conflicts.

And many of Africa's people felt they were unjustly condemned to be exploited and oppressed, generation after generation, since colonial rule had been replaced by an inequitable economic order on the global level, and sometimes by corrupt rulers and warlords at the local level.

In the decade since then, many people have been struggling to confront these three global challenges. Much has been achieved, but events have also presented us with new challenges–or rather, have given the old ones new form, or a sharper bite.

In the economic arena, both globalization and growth have continued apace.

Some developing countries, notably in Asia, have played a major role in this growth. Many millions of their people have thereby been released from the prison of perpetual poverty.

Meanwhile, at the level of development policy, the debate has advanced, moving from rival models to agreed targets. And the world has now recognized HIV/AIDS as a major challenge to development, and begun to confront it. I am proud of the role the United Nations has played in this. Development, and the Millennium Development Goals, now take pride of place in all our work.

But let's not delude ourselves. The Asian miracle is yet to be replicated in other parts of the world. And even within the most dynamic Asian countries, its benefits are far from equally shared.

By the same token, the Millennium Goals are unlikely to be achieved everywhere by 2015.

True, in many developing countries there is now a much better understanding of what good governance is, and why it's important. But many still fall short of it in practice.

True, there is progress on debt relief, as well as encouraging promises on aid and investment. But the "global partnership for development" is still more phrase than fact–especially in the all-important area of trade.

My friends, globalization is not a tide that lifts all boats. Even among those who the statistics tell us are benefiting, many are deeply insecure, and strongly resent the apparent complacency of those more fortunate than themselves.

So globalization, which in theory brings us all closer together, in practice risks driving us further apart.

Are we any more secure against the second challenge–the ravages of war?

Again, some statistics would tell us so. There are fewer inter-state conflicts than there used to be; and many civil wars have ended.

Here too, I am proud of the United Nations' role in this. And I am proud of what my fellow Africans have achieved in ending many of the conflicts that disfigured our continent.

But here too, we should be under no illusion.

In far too many parts of the world–especially the developing world–people are still exposed to brutal conflicts, fought with small but deadly weapons.

And people in all parts of the world are threatened–though some are more aware of it than others–by the spread of weapons of mass destruction It is shameful that last year's Summit Outcome does not contain even one word about non-proliferation and disarmament–basically because states could not agree which of the two should be given priority. It is high time to end this dispute, and tackle both tasks with the urgency they demand.

Moreover, just as some who benefit from globalization may feel threatened by it, so, many who are statistically safer from conflict do not feel safe.

For that, we have terrorism to thank. It kills and maims relatively few people, compared to other forms of violence and conflict. But it spreads fear and insecurity. And that in turn drives people to huddle together with those who share their beliefs or their way of life, while shunning those who appear "alien".

Thus, at the very time when international migration has brought millions of people of different creed or culture to live as fellow-citizens, the misconceptions and stereotypes underlying the idea of a 'clash of civilizations' have come to be more and more widely shared; and insensitivity towards other people's beliefs or sacred symbols–intentional or otherwise–is seized upon by those who seem eager to foment a new war of religion, this time on a global scale.

Moreover, this climate of fear and suspicion is constantly refuelled by the violence in the Middle East.

We might like to think of the Arab-Israeli conflict as just one regional conflict amongst many. But it is not. No other conflict carries such a powerful symbolic and emotional charge among people far removed from the battlefield.

As long as the Palestinians live under occupation, exposed to daily frustration and humiliation; and as long as Israelis are blown up in buses and in dance-halls: so long will passions everywhere be inflamed.

On one side, supporters of Israel feel that it is harshly judged, by standards that are not applied to its enemies–and too often this is true, particularly in some UN bodies.

On the other side, people are outraged by the disproportionate use of force against the Palestinians, and by Israel's continued occupation and confiscation of Arab land.

As long as the Security Council is unable to end this conflict, and the now nearly 40-year-old occupation, by bringing both sides to accept and implement its resolutions, so long will respect for the United Nations continue to decline. So long, too, will our impartiality be questioned. So long will our best efforts to resolve other conflicts be resisted, including those in Iraq and Afghanistan, whose peoples need our help just as badly, and are entitled to it. And so long will our devoted and courageous staff, instead of being protected by the blue flag, find themselves exposed to rage and violence, provoked by policies they neither control nor support.

But what about the third great challenge facing humanity–the challenge of the rule of law, and our rights and dignity as human beings? Here, too, there has been significant progress.

More rights have been enshrined in international treaties–and this Assembly is now about to codify the rights of a group who particularly need it: people who suffer from handicaps and disabilities.

More governments today are elected by, and are accountable to, those whom they govern.

Humanity has actually brought to justice some of those who committed the most heinous crimes against it.

And this Assembly, meeting last year at the highest level, has solemnly proclaimed the responsibility–of each individual State in the first instance, but ultimately of the whole international community, acting through the United Nations–to "protect populations from genocide, war crimes, ethnic cleansing and crimes against humanity".

And yet. And yet.

Every day, reports reach us of new laws broken; of new bestial crimes to which individuals and minority groups are subjected.

Even the necessary and legitimate struggle around the world against terrorism is used as a pretext to abridge or abrogate fundamental human rights, thereby ceding moral ground to the terrorists and helping them find new recruits.

Sadly, once again the biggest challenge comes from Africa–from Darfur, where the continued spectacle of men, women and children driven from their homes by murder, rape and the burning of their villages makes a mockery of our claim, as an international community, to shield people from the worst abuses.

In short, Madam President, the events of the last ten years have not resolved, but sharpened, the three great challenges I spoke of–an unjust world economy, world disorder, and widespread contempt for human rights and the rule of law. As a result, we face a world whose divisions threaten the very notion of an international community, upon which this institution stands.

And this is happening at the very time when, more than ever before, human beings throughout the world form a single society. So many of the challenges we face are global. They demand a global response, in which all peoples must play their part.

I deliberately say, "all peoples", echoing the preamble of our Charter, and not, "all states". It was clear to me ten years ago, and is even clearer now, that international relations are not a matter of States alone. They are relations between peoples, in which so-called "non-state actors" play a vital role, and can make a vital contribution. All must play their part in a true multilateral world order, with a renewed, dynamic United Nations at its centre.

Yes, I remain convinced that the only answer to this divided world must be a truly United Nations. Climate change, HIV/AIDS, fair trade, migration, human rights–all these issues, and many more, bring us back to that point. Addressing each is indispensable for each of us in our village, in our neighbourhood, and in our country. Yet each has acquired a global dimension that can only be reached by global action, agreed and coordinated through this most universal of institutions.

What matters is that the strong, as well as the weak, agree to be bound by the same rules, to treat each other with the same respect.

What matters is that all peoples accept the need to listen; to compromise; to take each other's views into account.

What matters is that they come together, not at cross purposes but with a common purpose: a common purpose–to shape their common destiny.

And that can only happen if peoples are bound together by something more than just a global market, or even a set of global rules.

Each of us must share the pain of all who suffer, and the joy of all who hope, wherever in the world they may live.

Each of us must earn the trust of his fellow men and women, no matter what their race, colour or creed, and learn to trust them in turn.

That is what the founders of this Organization believed in. It is what I believe in. It is what the vast majority of people in this world want to believe in.

And that is what has spurred the reforms and new ideas of the United Nations over the last frenetic decade. From peacekeeping to peacebuilding, from human rights to development and humanitarian relief, I have been lucky enough to preside over the Secretariat–and its wonderful, devoted staff–at a time when your ambitions for the Organization have sometimes seemed limitless–although your pocket books less so.

These last few weeks, especially, as I travelled through the Middle East, I saw again the legitimacy and the reach of the United Nations. Its indispensable role in securing the peace in Lebanon has reminded us all how powerful this Organization can be, when everyone wants it to succeed.

Madam President, dear friends:

This is the last time I shall have the honour of presenting my annual report to this Assembly. Let me conclude by thanking you all for allowing me to serve as Secretary-General during this remarkable decade.

Together we have pushed some big rocks to the top of the mountain, even if others have slipped from our grasp and rolled back. But this mountain with its bracing winds and global views is the best place on earth to be.

It's been difficult and challenging, but at times thrillingly rewarding. And while I look forward to resting my shoulder from those stubborn rocks in the next phase of my life, I know I shall miss the mountain. Yes, I shall miss what is, when all is said and done, the world's most exalting job. I yield my place to others with an obstinate feeling, a real obstinate feeling of hope for our common future.

Thank you very much.

★

Second Speech by: Kofi A. Annan

Topic: Role of Disarmament, Non-proliferation

Date: November 28, 2006 at Princeton University (US)

Let me begin by saying how delighted I am to have been invited to give this address by a School named after Woodrow Wilson, the great pioneer of multilateralism and advocate of world peace, who argued, among other things, for agreed international limits on deadly weapons.

Princeton is indissolubly linked with the memory of Albert Einstein and many other great scientists who played a role in making this country the first nuclear power. That makes it an especially appropriate setting for my address this evening, because my main theme is the danger of nuclear weapons, and the urgent need to confront that danger by preventing proliferation and promoting disarmament, both at once. I shall argue that these two objectives–disarmament and non-proliferation–are inextricably linked, and that to achieve progress on either front we must also advance on the other.

Almost everyone in today's world feels insecure, but not everyone feels insecure about the same thing. Different threats seem more urgent to people in different parts of the world.

Probably the largest number would give priority to economic and social threats, including poverty, environmental degradation and infectious disease.

Others might stress inter-state conflict; yet others internal conflict, including civil war. Many people–especially but not only in the developed world–would now put terrorism at the top of their list.

In truth, all these threats are interconnected, and all cut across national frontiers. We need common global strategies to deal with all of them–and indeed governments are coming together to work out and implement such strategies, in the UN and elsewhere. The one area where there is a total lack of any common strategy is the one that may well present the greatest danger of all: the area of nuclear weapons.

Why do I consider it the greatest danger? For three reasons:

First, nuclear weapons present a unique existential threat to all humanity.

Secondly, the nuclear non-proliferation regime now faces a major crisis of confidence. North Korea has withdrawn from the Nuclear Non-Proliferation Treaty (NPT), while India , Israel , and Pakistan have never joined it. There are, at least, serious questions about the nature of Iran 's nuclear programme. And this in turn raises questions about the legitimacy, and credibility, of the case-by-case approach to non-proliferation that the existing nuclear powers have adopted.

Thirdly, the rise of terrorism, with the danger that nuclear weapons might be acquired by terrorists, greatly increases the danger that they will be used.

Yet, despite the grave, all-encompassing nature of this threat, the governments of the world are addressing it selectively, not comprehensively.

In one way, that's understandable. The very idea of global self-annihilation is unbearable to think about. But that is no excuse. We must try to imagine the human and environmental consequences of a nuclear bomb exploding in one, or even in several, major world cities–or indeed of an all-out confrontation between two nuclear-armed states.

In focusing on nuclear weapons, I am not seeking to minimise the problem of chemical and biological ones, which are also weapons of mass destruction, and are banned under international treaties. Indeed, perhaps the most important, under-addressed threat relating to terrorism–one which acutely requires new thinking–is the threat of terrorists using a biological weapon.

But nuclear weapons are the most dangerous. Even a single bomb can destroy an entire city, as we know from the terrible example of Hiroshima and Nagasaki, and today there are bombs many times as powerful as those. These weapons pose a unique threat to humanity as a whole.

Forty years ago, understanding that this danger must be avoided at all costs, nearly all states in the world came together and forged a grand bargain, embodied in the NPT.

In essence, that treaty was a contract between the recognized nuclear-weapon states at that time and the rest of the international community. The nuclear-weapon states undertook to negotiate in good faith on nuclear disarmament, to prevent proliferation, and to facilitate the peaceful use of nuclear energy, while separately declaring that they would refrain from threatening non-nuclear-weapon states with nuclear weapons. In return, the rest committed themselves not to acquire or manufacture nuclear weapons, and to place all their nuclear activities under the verification of the International Atomic Energy Agency (IAEA). Thus the treaty was designed both to prevent proliferation and to advance disarmament, while assuring the right of all states, under specified conditions, to use nuclear energy for peaceful purposes.

From 1970–when it entered into force–until quite recently, the NPT was widely seen as a cornerstone of global security. It had confounded the dire predictions of its critics. Nuclear weapons did not–and still have not–spread to dozens of states, as John F. Kennedy and others predicted in the 1960s. In fact, more states have given up their ambitions for nuclear weapons than have acquired them.

And yet in recent years the NPT has come under withering criticism–because the international community has been unable to agree how to apply it to specific crises in South Asia, the Korean peninsula and the Middle East ; and because a few states parties to the treaty are allegedly pursuing their own nuclear-weapons capabilities.

Twice in 2005, governments had a chance to strengthen the Treaty's foundations–first at the Review conference in May, then at the World Summit in September. Both times they failed–

essentially because they couldn't agree whether non-proliferation or disarmament should come first.

The advocates of "non-proliferation first"–mainly nuclear-weapon states and their supporters–believe the main danger arises not from nuclear weapons as such, but from the character of those who possess them, and therefore from the spread of nuclear weapons to new states and to non-state actors (so-called "horizontal proliferation"). The nuclear-weapon states say they have carried out significant disarmament since the end of the Cold War, but that their responsibility for international peace and security requires them to maintain a nuclear deterrent.

Disarmament first advocates, on the other hand, say that the world is most imperilled by existing nuclear arsenals and their continual improvement (so-called "vertical proliferation"). Many non-nuclear-weapon states accuse the nuclear-weapon states of retreating from commitments they made in 1995 (when the NPT was extended indefinitely) and reiterated as recently as the year 2000. For these countries, the NPT "grand bargain" has become a swindle. They note that the UN Security Council has often described the proliferation of weapons of mass destruction as a threat to international peace and security, but has never declared that nuclear weapons in and of themselves are such a threat. They see no serious movement towards nuclear disarmament, and claim that the lack of such movement presages a permanent 'apartheid' between nuclear 'haves' and 'have-nots'.

Both sides in this debate feel that the existence of four additional states with nuclear weapons, outside the NPT, serves only to sharpen their argument.

Arms build-ups can give rise to threats leading to conflict; and political conflicts can motivate the acquisition of arms. Efforts are needed both to reduce arms and to reduce conflict. Likewise, efforts are needed to achieve both disarmament and non-proliferation.

Yet each side waits for the other to move. The result is that 'mutually assured destruction' has been replaced by mutually assured paralysis. This sends a terrible signal of disunity and waning respect for the Treaty's authority. It creates a vacuum that can be exploited.

I said earlier this year that we are 'sleepwalking towards disaster'. In truth, it is worse than that–we are asleep at the controls of a fast-moving aircraft. Unless we wake up and take control, the outcome is all too predictable.

An aircraft, of course, can remain airborne only if both wings are in working order. We cannot choose between non-proliferation and disarmament. We must tackle both tasks with the urgency they demand.

Allow me to offer my thoughts to each side in turn.

To those who insist on disarmament first, I say this:

Proliferation is not a threat only, or even mainly, to those who already have nuclear weapons. The more fingers there are on nuclear triggers, and the more those fingers belong to leaders of unstable states–or, even worse, non-state actors–the greater the threat to all humankind.

Lack of progress on disarmament is no excuse for not addressing the dangers of proliferation. No state should imagine that, by pushing ahead with a nuclear-weapon programme, it can pose as a defender of the NPT; still less that it will persuade others to disarm.

I urge all states to give credit where it is due. Acknowledge disarmament whenever it does occur. Applaud the moves which nuclear-weapon states have made, whether unilaterally or through negotiation, to reduce nuclear arsenals or prevent their expansion.

Recognize that the nuclear-weapon states have virtually stopped producing new fissile material for weapons, and are maintaining moratoria on nuclear tests.

Likewise, support even small steps to contain proliferation, such as efforts to improve export controls on goods needed to make weapons of mass destruction, as mandated by Security Council Resolution 1540.

And please support the efforts of t he Director-General of the IAEA and others to find ways of guaranteeing that all states have access to fuel and services for their civilian nuclear programmes without spreading sensitive technology. Countries must be able to meet their growing energy needs through such programmes, but we cannot afford a world where more and more countries develop the most sensitive phases of the nuclear fuel cycle themselves.

Finally, do not encourage, or allow, any state to make its compliance with initiatives to eliminate nuclear weapons, or halt their proliferation, conditional on concessions from other states on other issues. The preservation of human life on this planet is too important to be used as a hostage.

To those who insist on non-proliferation first, I say this:

True, there has been some progress on nuclear disarmament since the end of the Cold War. Some states have removed many nuclear weapons from deployment, and eliminated whole classes of nuclear delivery systems. The US and Russia have agreed to limit the number of strategic nuclear weapons they deploy, and have removed non-strategic ones from ships and submarines; the US Congress refused to fund the so-called "bunker-buster" bomb; most nuclear test sites have been closed; and there are national moratoria on nuclear tests, while three nuclear-weapon states–France, Russia and the UK–have ratified the Comprehensive Nuclear-Test-Ban Treaty.

Yet stockpiles remain alarmingly high: 27,000 nuclear weapons reportedly remain in service, of which about 12,000 are actively deployed.

Some states seem to believe they need fewer weapons, but smaller and more useable ones–and even to have embraced the notion of using such weapons in conflict. All of the NPT nuclear-weapon states are modernizing their nuclear arsenals or their delivery systems. They should not imagine that this will be accepted as compatible with the NPT. Everyone will see it for what it is: a euphemism for nuclear re-armament.

Nor is it clear how these states propose to deal with the four nuclear-weapon-capable states outside the NPT. They warn against a nuclear domino effect if this or that country is allowed to acquire a nuclear capability, but they do not seem to know how to prevent it, or how to respond to it once it has happened. Surely they should at least consider attempting a "reverse domino effect", in which systematic and sustained reductions in nuclear arsenals would devalue the currency of nuclear weapons, and encourage others to follow suit.

Instead, by clinging to and modernizing their own arsenals, even when there is no obvious threat to their national security that nuclear weapons could deter, nuclear-weapon states encourage others–particularly those that do face real threats in their own region–to regard nuclear weapons as essential, both to their security and to their status. It would be much easier to confront proliferators if the very existence of nuclear weapons were universally acknowledged as dangerous and ultimately illegitimate.

Similarly, states that wish to discourage others from undertaking nuclear or missile tests could argue their case much more convincingly if they themselves moved quickly to bring the Comprehensive Nuclear-Test-Ban Treaty into force, halt their own missile testing, and negotiate a robust multilateral instrument regulating missiles. Such steps would do more than anything else to advance the cause of non-proliferation.

Important powers such as Argentina , Brazil , Germany and Japan have shown, by refusing to develop them, that nuclear weapons are not essential to either security or status. South Africa destroyed its arsenal and joined the NPT. Belarus, Ukraine and Kazakhstan gave up nuclear weapons from the former Soviet nuclear arsenal. And Libya has abandoned its nuclear and chemical weapons programmes. The nuclear weapon states have applauded all these examples. They should follow them.

Finally, governments and civil society in many countries are increasingly questioning the relevance of the Cold War doctrine of nuclear deterrence–the rationale used by all states that possess nuclear weapons–in an age of growing threats from non-state actors. Do we not need, instead, to develop agreed strategies for preventing proliferation?

For all these reasons, I call on all the states with nuclear weapons to develop concrete plans–with specific timetables–for implementing their disarmament commitments. And I urge them to make a joint declaration of intent to achieve the progressive elimination of all nuclear weapons, under strict and effective international control.

In short, my friends, the only way forward is to make progress on both fronts–non-proliferation and disarmament–at once. And we will not achieve this unless at the same time we deal/effectively with the threat of terrorism, as well as the threats, both real and rhetorical, which drive particular states or regimes to seek security, however misguidedly, by developing or acquiring nuclear weapons.

It is a complex and daunting task, which calls for leadership, for the establishment of trust, for dialogue and negotiation. But first of all, we need a renewed debate, which must be inclusive, must respect the norms of international negotiations, and must reaffirm the multilateral approach–Woodrow Wilson's approach, firmly grounded in international institutions, treaties, rules, and norms of appropriate behaviour.

Let me conclude by appealing to young people everywhere, since there are–I am glad to see–so many of them here today.

My dear young friends, you are already admirably engaged in the struggle for global development, for human rights, and to protect the environment. Please bring your energy and imagination to this debate. Help us to seize control of the rogue aircraft on which humanity has embarked, and bring it to a safe landing before it is too late.

Thank you very much.

■

Biographical Sketch: Mohandas Karamchand Gandhi (October 2, 1869–January 30, 1948) was a major political and spiritual leader of India. He was the leader of the Indian independence movement. He is recognised as the Father of the Nation. He was the pioneer of Satyagraha–the resistance of tyranny through mass civil disobedience. He propagated *ahimsa* or total non-violence.

October 2nd, his birthday, is commemorated each year as Gandhi Jayanti, and is a national holiday.

Speech By: Mahatma Gandhi

Topic: Quit India

Date: August 8, 1942

Before you discuss the resolution, let me place before you one or two things, I want you to understand two things very clearly and to consider them from the same point of view from which I am placing them before you. I ask you to consider it from my point of view, because if you approve of it, you will be enjoined to carry out all I say. It will be a great responsibility. There are people who ask me whether I am the same man that I was in 1920, or whether there has been any change in me. You are right in asking that question.

Let me, however, hasten to assure that I am the same Gandhi as I was in 1920. I have not changed in any fundamental respect. I attach the same importance to non-violence that I did then. If at all, my emphasis on it has grown stronger. There is no real contradiction between the present resolution and my previous writings and utterances.

Occasions like the present do not occur in everybody's and but rarely in anybody's life. I want you to know and feel that there is nothing but purest *Ahimsa* in all that I am saying and doing today. The draft resolution of the Working Committee is based on Ahimsa, the contemplated struggle similarly has its roots in Ahimsa. If, therefore, there is any among you who has lost faith in Ahimsa or is wearied of it, let him not vote for this resolution.

Let me explain my position clearly. God has vouchsafed to me a priceless gift in the weapon of Ahimsa. I and my Ahimsa are on our trail today. If in the present crisis, when the earth is being scorched by the flames of Himsa and crying for deliverance, I failed to make use of the God given talent, God will not forgive me and I shall be judged un-wrongly of the great gift. I must act now. I may not hesitate and merely look on, when Russia and China are threatened.

Ours is not a drive for power, but purely a non-violent fight for India's independence. In a violent struggle, a successful general has been often known to affect a military coup and to set up a dictatorship. But under the Congress scheme of things, essentially non-violent as it is, there can be no room for dictatorship. A non-violent soldier of freedom will covet nothing for himself, he fights only for the freedom of his country. The Congress is unconcerned as to who will rule, when freedom is attained. The power, when it comes, will belong to the people of India, and it will be for them to decide to whom it placed in the entrusted. May be that the reins will be placed in the hands of the Parsis, for instance-as I would love to see happen-or they may be handed to some others whose names are not heard in the Congress today. It will not be for you then to object saying, 'This community is microscopic. That party did not play its due part in the freedom's struggle; why should it have all the power?' Ever since its inception the Congress has kept itself meticulously free of the communal taint. It has thought always in terms of the whole nation and has acted accordingly ...

I know how imperfect our Ahimsa is and how far away we are still from the ideal, but in Ahimsa there is no final failure or defeat. I have faith, therefore, that if, in spite of our shortcomings, the big thing does happen, it will be because God wanted to help us by crowning with success our silent, unremitting Sadhana for the last twenty-two years.

I believe that in the history of the world, there has not been a more genuinely democratic struggle for freedom than ours. I read Carlyle's French Resolution while I was in prison, and Pundit Jawaharlal has told me something about the Russian revolution. But it is my conviction that inasmuch as these struggles were fought with the weapon of violence they failed to realize the democratic ideal. In the democracy which I have envisaged, a democracy established by non-violence, there will be equal freedom for all. Everybody will be his own master. It is to join a struggle for such democracy that I invite you today. Once you realize this you will forget the differences between the Hindus and Muslims, and think of yourselves as Indians only, engaged in the common struggle for independence.

Then, there is the question of your attitude towards the British. I have noticed that there is hatred towards the British among the people. The people say they are disgusted with their behaviour. The people make no distinction between British imperialism and the British people. To them, the two are one this hatred would even make them welcome the Japanese. It is most dangerous. It means that they will exchange one slavery for another. We must get rid of this feeling. Our quarrel is not with the British people, we fight their imperialism. The proposal for the withdrawal of British power did not come out of anger. It came to enable India to play its due part at the present critical juncture It is not a happy position for a big country like India to be merely helping with money and material obtained willy-nilly from her while the United Nations are conducting the war. We cannot evoke the true spirit of sacrifice and velour, so long as we are not free. I know the British Government will not be able to withhold freedom from us, when we have made enough self-sacrifice. We must, therefore, purge ourselves of hatred. Speaking for myself, I can say that I have never felt any hatred. As a matter of fact, I feel myself to be a greater friend of the British now than ever before. One reason is that they are today in distress. My very friendship, therefore, demands that I should try to save them from their mistakes. As I view the situation, they are on the brink of an abyss. It, therefore, becomes my duty to warn them of their danger even though it may, for the time being, anger them to the point of cutting off the friendly hand that is stretched out to help them. People may laugh, nevertheless that is my claim. At a time when I may have to launch the biggest struggle of my life, I may not harbour hatred against anybody.

■

Biographical Sketch: Samuel Langhorne Clemens (November 30, 1835–April 21, 1910) was an American humorist, satirist, writer, and lecturer. He is better known by the pen name Mark Twain. His most noted novels include *Adventures of Huckleberry Finn* and *The Adventures of Tom Sawyer*. He is also known for his quotations. He enjoyed immense public popularity, and his keen wit and incisive satire earned him praise from both critics and peers. He has also been called 'the father of American literature' by author William Faulkner.

Speech By: Mark Twain

Topic: Votes for Women

Date: January 20, 1901

Ladies and Gentlemen–It is a small help that I can afford, but it is just such help that one can give as coming from the heart through the mouth. The report of Mr. Meyer was admirable, and I was as interested in it as you have been. Why, I'm twice as old as he, and I've had so much experience that I would say to him, when he makes his appeal for help: "Don't make it for today or tomorrow, but collect the money on the spot."

We are all creatures of sudden impulse. We must be worked up by steam, as it were. Get them to write their wills now, or it may be too late by-and-by. Fifteen or twenty years ago I had an experience I shall never forget. I got into a church which was crowded by a sweltering and panting multitude. The city missionary of our town–Hartford–made a telling appeal for help.

He told of personal experiences among the poor in cellars and top lofts requiring instances of devotion and help. The poor are always good to the poor. When a person with his millions gives a hundred thousand dollars it makes a great noise in the world, but he does not miss it; it's the widow's mite that makes no noise but does the best work.

I remember on that occasion in the Hartford church the collection was being taken up. The appeal had so stirred me that I could hardly wait for the hat or plate to come my way. I had four hundred dollars in my pocket, and I was anxious to drop it in the plate and wanted to borrow more. But the plate was so long in coming my way that the fever-heat of beneficence was going down lower and lower–going down at the rate of a hundred dollars a minute. The plate was passed too late. When it finally came to me, my enthusiasm had gone down so much that I kept my four hundred dollars–and stole a dime from the plate. So, you see, time sometimes leads to crime. Oh, many a time have I thought of that and regretted it, and I adjure you all to give while the fever is on you.

Referring to woman's sphere in life, I'll say that woman is always right. For twenty-five years I've been a woman's rights man. I have always believed, long before my mother died, that, with her gray hairs and admirable intellect, perhaps she knew as much as I did. Perhaps she knew as much about voting as I. I should like to see the time come when women shall help to make the laws. I should like to see that whiplash, the ballot, in the hands of women. As for this city's government, I don't want to say much, except that it is a shame–a shame; but if I should live twenty-five years longer–and there is no reason why I shouldn't–I think I'll see women handle the ballot. If women had the ballot to-day, the state of things in this town would not exist.

If all the women in this town had a vote today they would elect a mayor at the next election, and they would rise in their might and change the awful state of things now existing here.

■

Biographical Sketch: Martin Luther King, Jr. (January 15, 1929–April 4, 1968) was the most popular leader of the American civil rights movement. He was a political activist and one of America's greatest orators. In 1964, he became the youngest man to be awarded the Nobel Peace Prize, for his work as a peacemaker, promoting non-violence and equal treatment for different races. He was assassinated in Memphis, Tennessee on April 4, 1968. He was posthumously awarded the Presidential Medal of Freedom by Jimmy Carter in 1977. Martin Luther King Day was established as a United States holiday in his honour in 1986. While alive, he often called for personal responsibility in fostering world peace. His most influential and well-known public address is the 'I Have a Dream' speech, delivered on the steps of the Lincoln Memorial in Washington, D.C. in 1963.

Speech By: Martin Luther King, Jr.

Topic: I Have a Dream

Date: August 28, 1963

I am happy to join with you today in what will go down in history as the greatest demonstration for freedom in the history of our nation.

Five score years ago, a great American, in whose symbolic shadow we stand today, signed the Emancipation Proclamation. This momentous decree came as a great beacon light of hope to millions of Negro slaves who had been seared in the flames of withering injustice. It came as a joyous daybreak to end the long night of their captivity.

But one hundred years later, the Negro still is not free. One hundred years later, the life of the Negro is still sadly crippled by the manacles of segregation and the chains of discrimination. One hundred years later, the Negro lives on a lonely island of poverty in the midst of a vast ocean of material prosperity. One hundred years later, the Negro is still languished in the corners of American society and finds himself an exile in his own land. And so we've come here today to dramatize a shameful condition.

In a sense we've come to our nation's capital to cash a check. When the architects of our republic wrote the magnificent words of the Constitution and the Declaration of Independence, they were signing a promissory note to which every American was to fall heir. This note was a promise that all men, yes, black men as well as white men, would be guaranteed the "unalienable Rights" of "Life, Liberty and the pursuit of Happiness." It is obvious today that America has defaulted on this promissory note, insofar as her citizens of color are concerned. Instead of honoring this sacred obligation, America has given the Negro people a bad check, a check which has come back marked "insufficient funds."

But we refuse to believe that the bank of justice is bankrupt. We refuse to believe that there are insufficient funds in the great vaults of opportunity of this nation. And so, we've come to cash this check, a check that will give us upon demand the riches of freedom and the security of justice.

We have also come to this hallowed spot to remind America of the fierce urgency of Now. This is no time to engage in the luxury of cooling off or to take the tranquilizing drug of gradualism. Now is the time to make real the promises of democracy. Now is the time to rise from the dark and desolate valley of segregation to the sunlit path of racial justice. Now is the time to lift our nation from the quicksands of racial injustice to the solid rock of brotherhood. Now is the time to make justice a reality for all of God's children.

It would be fatal for the nation to overlook the urgency of the moment. This sweltering summer of the Negro's legitimate discontent will not pass until there is an invigorating autumn of freedom and equality. Nineteen sixty–three is not an end, but a beginning. And those who hope that the Negro needed to blow off steam and will now be content will have a rude awakening if the nation returns to business as usual. And there will be neither rest nor tranquility in America until the Negro is granted his citizenship rights. The whirlwinds of revolt will continue to shake the foundations of our nation until the bright day of justice emerges.

But there is something that I must say to my people, who stand on the warm threshold which leads into the palace of justice: In the process of gaining our rightful place, we must not be guilty of wrongful deeds. Let us not seek to satisfy our thirst for freedom by drinking from the cup of bitterness and hatred. We must forever conduct our struggle on the high plane of dignity and discipline. We must not allow our creative protest to degenerate into physical violence. Again and again, we must rise to the majestic heights of meeting physical force with soul force.

The marvelous new militancy which has engulfed the Negro community must not lead us to a distrust of all white people, for many of our white brothers, as evidenced by their presence here today, have come to realize that their destiny is tied up with our destiny. And they have come to realize that their freedom is inextricably bound to our freedom.

We cannot walk alone.

And as we walk, we must make the pledge that we shall always march ahead.

We cannot turn back.

There are those who are asking the devotees of civil rights, "When will you be satisfied?" We can never be satisfied as long as the Negro is the victim of the unspeakable horrors of police brutality. We can never be satisfied as long as our bodies, heavy with the fatigue of travel, cannot gain lodging in the motels of the highways and the hotels of the cities. *We cannot be satisfied as long as the Negro's basic mobility is from a smaller ghetto to a larger one. We can never be satisfied as long as our children are stripped of their self-hood and robbed of their dignity by a sign stating: "For Whites Only."* We cannot be satisfied as long as a Negro in Mississippi cannot vote and a Negro in New York believes he has nothing for which to vote. No, no, we are not satisfied, and we will not be satisfied until "justice rolls down like waters, and righteousness like a mighty stream."

I am not unmindful that some of you have come here out of great trials and tribulations. Some of you have come fresh from narrow jail cells. And some of you have come from areas where your quest–quest for freedom left you battered by the storms of persecution and staggered by the winds of police brutality. You have been the veterans of creative suffering. Continue to work with the faith that unearned suffering is redemptive. Go back to Mississippi, go back to Alabama, go back to South Carolina, go back to Georgia, go back to Louisiana, go back to the slums and ghettos of our northern cities, knowing that somehow this situation can and will be changed.

Let us not wallow in the valley of despair, I say to you today, my friends.

And so even though we face the difficulties of today and tomorrow, I still have a dream. It is a dream deeply rooted in the American dream.

I have a dream that one day this nation will rise up and live out the true meaning of its creed: "We hold these truths to be self-evident, that all men are created equal."

I have a dream that one day on the red hills of Georgia, the sons of former slaves and the sons of former slave owners will be able to sit down together at the table of brotherhood.

I have a dream that one day even the state of Mississippi, a state sweltering with the heat of injustice, sweltering with the heat of oppression, will be transformed into an oasis of freedom and justice.

I have a dream that my four little children will one day live in a nation where they will not be judged by the color of their skin but by the content of their character.

I have a dream today!

I have a dream that one day, down in Alabama, with its vicious racists, with its governor having his lips dripping with the words of "interposition" and "nullification"–one day right there in Alabama little black boys and black girls will be able to join hands with little white boys and white girls as sisters and brothers.

I have a dream today!

I have a dream that one day every valley shall be exalted, and every hill and mountain shall be made low, the rough places will be made plain, and the crooked places will be made straight; "and the glory of the Lord shall be revealed and all flesh shall see it together."

This is our hope, and this is the faith that I go back to the South with.

With this faith, we will be able to hew out of the mountain of despair a stone of hope. With this faith, we will be able to transform the jangling discords of our nation into a beautiful symphony of brotherhood. With this faith, we will be able to work together, to pray together, to struggle together, to go to jail together, to stand up for freedom together, knowing that we will be free one day.

And this will be the day–this will be the day when all of God's children will be able to sing with new meaning:

My country 'tis of thee, sweet land of liberty, of thee I sing.

Land where my fathers died, land of the Pilgrim's pride,

From every mountainside, let freedom ring!

And if America is to be a great nation, this must become true.

And so let freedom ring from the prodigious hilltops of New Hampshire.

Let freedom ring from the mighty mountains of New York.

Let freedom ring from the heightening Alleghenies of Pennsylvania.

Let freedom ring from the snow-capped Rockies of Colorado.

Let freedom ring from the curvaceous slopes of California.

But not only that:

Let freedom ring from Stone Mountain of Georgia.

Let freedom ring from Lookout Mountain of Tennessee.

Let freedom ring from every hill and molehill of Mississippi.

From every mountainside, let freedom ring.

And when this happens, when we allow freedom ring, when we let it ring from every village and every hamlet, from every state and every city, we will be able to speed up that day when all of God's children, black men and white men, Jews and Gentiles, Protestants and Catholics, will be able to join hands and sing in the words of the old Negro spiritual:

Free at last! Free at last!

Thank God Almighty, we are free at last!

■

Biographical Sketch: Mother Teresa (August 26, 1910–September 5, 1997) was born as Agnes Gonxha Bojaxhiu in the Kosovo Province of the Ottoman Empire to Albanian parents. Raised as a Catholic by her parents, her father died when she was about eight years old. At the age of 18, she joined the Sisters of Loreto, an Irish community of nuns with a mission in Calcutta. After a few months' training in Dublin, she was sent to India. She founded the Missionaries of Charity and won the Nobel Peace Prize in 1979 for her humanitarian work. She ministered to the needs of the poor, sick, orphaned and dying of Calcutta, India.

Speech By: Mother Teresa of Calcutta

Topic: National Prayer Breakfast Speech Against Abortion

Date: February 3, 1994 in Washington

On the last day, Jesus will say to those at his right hand, "Come, enter the Kingdom. For I was hungry and you gave me food, I was thirsty and you gave me drink, I was sick and you visited me."

Then Jesus will turn to those on his left hand and say, "Depart from me because I was hungry and you did not feed me, I was thirsty and you did not give me drink, I was sick and you did not visit me."

These will ask him "When did we see you hungry, or thirsty, or sick, and did not come to your help?"

And Jesus will answer them, "Whatever you neglected to do unto the least of these you neglected to do unto me!"

Let us thank God for the opportunity He has given us today to have come here to pray together. We have come here especially to pray for peace, joy and love. We are reminded that Jesus came to bring the good news to the poor. He had told us what that good news was when he said, "My peace I leave with you, My Peace I give unto you." He came not to give the peace of the world, which is only that we don't bother each other. He came to give peace of the heart which comes from loving, from doing good to others.

And God loved the world so much that he gave His Son. God gave His Son to the Virgin Mary, and what did she do with Him? As soon as Jesus came into Mary's life, immediately she went in haste to give that good news. And as she came into the house of her cousin, Elizabeth, Scripture tells us that the unborn child–the child in the womb of Elizabeth–leapt with joy.

While still in the womb of Mary, Jesus brought peace to John the Baptist, who leapt for joy in the womb of Elizabeth. And as if that were not enough–as if it were not enough that God the Son should become one of us and bring peace and joy while still in the womb–Jesus also died on the Cross to show that greater love.

He died for you and for me, and for that leper and for that man dying of hunger and that naked person lying in the street–not only of Calcutta, but of Africa, of everywhere. Our Sisters serve these people in 105 countries throughout the world. Jesus insisted that we love one another as He loves each one of us. Jesus gave His life to love us, and He tells us very clearly, "Love as I have loved you."

Jesus died on the Cross because that is what it took for Him to do good for us–to save us from our selfishness and sin. He gave up everything to do the Father's will, to show us that we, too, must be willing to give everything to do God's will, to love one another as He loves each of us.

St. John says you are a liar if you love God and you don't love your neighbour. How can you love God whom you do not see, if you do not love your neighbour whom you see, whom you touch, with whom you live?

Jesus makes Himself the hungry one, the naked one, the homeless one, the unwanted one, and He says, "You did it to me."

I can never forget the experience I had in visiting a home where they kept all these old parents of sons and daughters who had just put them into an institution and, maybe, forgotten them. I saw that in the home these old people had everything: good food, comfortable place, television–everything. But everyone was looking toward the door. And I did not see a single one with a smile on his face.

I turned to Sister and I asked, "Why do these people, who have every comfort here–why are they all looking toward the door? Why are they not smiling?" (I am so used to seeing the smiles on our people. Even the dying ones smile.) And Sister said, "This is the way it is, nearly every day. They are expecting that a son or daughter will come visit them.

See, this neglect to love brings spiritual poverty. Maybe in our family we have someone who is feeling lonely, who is feeling sick, who is feeling worried. Are we willing to give until it hurts, in order to be with our families? Or do we put our own interests first?

I was surprised in the West to see so many boys and girls given to drugs. And I tried to find out why. Why is it like that when those in the West have so many more things than those in the East? And the answer was: "Because there was no one in the family to receive them."

Our children depend on us for everything: their health, their nutrition, their security, their coming to know and love God. For all of this, they look to us with trust, hope and expectation. But often father and mother are so busy that they have no time for their children, or perhaps they are not even married, or have given up on their marriage. So the children go to the streets, and get involved in drugs, or other things.

We are talking of love of the child, which is where love and peace must begin.

But I feel that the greatest destroyer of peace today is abortion, because it is a war against the child–a direct killing of the innocent child–murder by the mother herself. And if we accept that a mother can kill her own child, how can we tell other people not to kill one another?

How do we persuade a woman not to have an abortion? As always, we must persuade her with love. The father of that child, whoever he is, must also give until it hurts. By abortion, the mother does not learn to love, but kills even her own child to solve her problems. And by abortion, the father is told that he does not have to take any responsibility at all for the child he has brought into the world.

Any country that accepts abortion is not teaching the people to love, but to use any violence to get what they want. That is why the greatest destroyer of love and peace is abortion.

And for this I appeal in India and I appeal everywhere: "Let us bring the child back." The child is God's gift to the family. Each child is created in the special image and likeness of God for greater things–to love and to be loved. This is the only way that our children are the only hope for the future. As other people are called to God, only their children can take their places.

But what does God say to us? He says, "Even if a mother could forget her child, I will not forget you. I have carved you in the palm of My hand." We are carved in the palm of His hand - that unborn child has been carved in the hand of God from conception, and is called by God to love and to be loved, not only now in this life, but forever. God can never forget us.

From our children's home in Calcutta alone, we have saved over 3,000 children from abortion. These children have brought such love and joy to their adopting parents, and have grown up so full of love and joy! I know that couples have to plan their family, and for that there is natural family planning, not contraception. A husband or a wife must turn their attention to each other, as happens in natural family planning, and not to self, as happens in contraception. Once that living love is destroyed by contraception, abortion follows very easily.

The poor are very great people. They can teach us so many beautiful things. Once one of them came to thank us for teaching them natural family planning, and said: "You people who have practiced chastity, you are the best people to teach us natural family planning, because it is nothing more than self-control out of love for each other." And what this poor person said is very true.

These poor people maybe have nothing to eat, maybe they have no home to live in, but they can still be great people when they are spiritually rich. Those who are materially poor can be wonderful people.

One evening, we went out and we picked up four people from the street. And one of them was in the most terrible condition. I told the Sisters: "You take care of the other three. I will take care of the one who looks worse." So I did for her all that my love can do. I put her in bed, and there was a beautiful smile on her face. She took hold of my hand, and she said one thing only: "Thank you." Then she died.

I could not help but examine my conscience before her. I asked, "What would I say if I were in her place?" And my answer was very simple. I would have tried to draw a little attention to myself. I would have said, "I am hungry, I am dying, I am cold, I am in pain," or something like that. But she gave me much more - she gave me her grateful love. And she died with a smile on her face.

Then there was a man we picked up from a drain, half eaten by worms. And after we had brought him to the home, he only said, "I have lived like an animal in the street, but I am going to die as an angel, loved and cared for." Then after we had removed all the worms from this body, all he said–with a big smile–was: "Sister, I am going home to God." And he died.

It was so wonderful to see the greatness of that man, who could speak like that without blaming anybody, without comparing anything. Like an angel - this is the greatness of people who are spiritually rich, even when they are materially poor.

And so here I am talking with you. I want you to find the poor here, right in your own home first. And begin love there. Bear the good news to your own people first. And find out about your next-door neighbours. Do you know who they are?

I had the most extraordinary experience of love of a neighbour from a Hindu family. A gentlemen came to our house and said, "Mother Teresa, there is a family who have not eaten for so long. Do something." So I took some rice and went there immediately. And I saw the children, their eyes shining with hunger. (I don't know if you have ever seen hunger, but I have seen it very often.) And the mother of the family took the rice I gave her.

"Where did you go? What did you do?" And she gave me a very simple answer: "They are hungry also." What struck me was that she knew. And who were "they?" A Muslim family. And she knew. I didn't bring any more rice that evening. I wanted them–Hindus and Muslims–to enjoy the joy of sharing.

Because I talk so much of giving with a smile, once a professor from the United States asked me, "Are you married?" And I said, "Yes, and I find it sometimes very difficult to smile at my spouse–Jesus–because He can be very demanding. Sometimes this is really something true. And there is where love comes in - when it is demanding, and yet we can give it with joy.

If we remember that God loves us, and that we can love others as He loves us, then America can become a sign of peace for the world. From here, a sign of care for the weakest of the weak–the unborn child–must go out to the world. If you become a burning light of justice and peace in the world, then really you will be true to what the founders of this country stood for.

God bless you!

■

Biographical Sketch: Napoleon Bonaparte (August 15, 1769–May 5, 1821) was a general during the French Revolution. Through his military exploits and ruthless efficiency, he rose from obscurity to become Napoleon I, Empereur des Francais (Emperor of the French). He decided on a military career when he was a child, winning a scholarship to a French military academy. His meteoric rise shocked not only France but all of Europe, and his military conquests threatened the stability of the world. He was one of the greatest military commanders in history and has also been portrayed as a power hungry conqueror.

Speech By: Napoleon Bonaparte

Topic: Congratulating troops on victory following the battle of Austerlitz

Date: December 2, 1805

Soldiers, I am pleased with you!

You have, on this day of Austerlitz, justified all that I looked for from your fearlessness. You have adorned your eagles with an everlasting glory. An army of 100,000 men, under the command of the Emperors of Russia and Austria, has been, within less than four hours, cut to pieces or disbanded. Those which escaped your blades are drowned in the lakes. Forty battle flags, the standard of the Russian imperial guard, 120 artillery pieces, twenty generals, and more than 30,000 prisoners, are the results of this day for all time renowned. This infantry so vaunted, and in numbers superior, could not resist you, and henceforth you have no rivals from which to fear. Thus, in two months, this third coalition has been vanquished and disbanded. Peace cannot be far away; but, as I promised my people before crossing the Rhine, I shall make only that peace that will give guaranties to us and rewards to our allies.

Soldiers, when the French people placed the imperial crown upon my head, I entrusted myself to you to keep it forever in those rays of glory which alone make it worthy in my eyes. But at that same moment, our enemies thought to destroy and dishonour it! And this crown of iron, conquered with the blood of so many Frenchmen, they wanted to compel me to place it upon the head of our most cruel enemies!

Rash and senseless endeavour, which, upon the very anniversary of the crowning of your Emperor, you have dashed and confounded. You have taught them that it is easier to defy and to threaten us, than to defeat us!

Soldiers, when all that is necessary to assure the happiness and prosperity of your fatherland has been accomplished, I shall bring you back to France. There, you will be object of my most tender care. My people shall greet your return with joy, and it will be enough for you to say "I was at the Battle of Austerlitz," that the reply shall be, "Here is a brave man".

■

Biographical Sketch: Pope John Paul II (May 18, 1920–April 2, 2005) reigned as Pope of the Catholic Church and Sovereign of the State of the Vatican City from October 16, 1978, until his death. He was one of the most beloved popes in history among Catholics and non-Catholics alike. His early reign was marked by his opposition to communism, and he is often credited as one of the forces which contributed to its collapse in Eastern Europe. He was notable for speaking against war, fascism, dictatorship, materialism, abortion, contraception, relativism, unrestrained capitalism, and what he regarded as the 'culture of death'.

Speech By: Pope John Paul II

Topic: The Holocaust Speech

Date: March 23, 2000 at Israel's Holocaust Memorial

The words of the ancient Psalm, rise from our hearts: "I have become like a broken vessel. I hear the whispering of many–terror on every side–as they scheme together against me, as they plot to take my life. But I trust in you, O Lord: I say, 'you are my God.'"

In this place of memories, the mind and heart and soul feel an extreme need for silence. Silence in which to remember. Silence in which to try to make some sense of the memories which come flooding back. Silence because there are no words strong enough to deplore the terrible tragedy of the Shoah.

My own personal memories are of all that happened when the Nazis occupied Poland during the war. I remember my Jewish friends and neighbours, some of whom perished, while others survived. I have come to Yad Vashem to pay homage to the millions of Jewish people who, stripped of everything, especially of human dignity, were murdered in the Holocaust. More than half a century has passed, but the memories remain.

Here, as at Auschwitz and many other places in Europe, we are overcome by the echo of the heart-rending laments of so many. Men, women and children, cry out to us from the depths of the horror that they knew. How can we fail to heed their cry? No one can forget or ignore what happened. No one can diminish its scale.

We wish to remember. But we wish to remember for a purpose, namely to ensure that never again will evil prevail, as it did for the millions of innocent victims of Nazism.

How could man have such utter contempt for man? Because he had reached the point of contempt for God. Only a godless ideology could plan and carry out the extermination of a whole people.

The honour given to the 'Just Gentiles' by the state of Israel at Yad Vashem for having acted heroically to save Jews, sometimes to the point of giving their own lives, is a recognition that not even in the darkest hour is every light extinguished. That is why the Psalms and the entire Bible, though well aware of the human capacity for evil, also proclaims that evil will not have the last word.

Out of the depths of pain and sorrow, the believer's heart cries out: "I trust in you, O Lord: 'I say, you are my God.'"

Jews and Christians share an immense spiritual patrimony, flowing from God's self-revelation. Our religious teachings and our spiritual experience demand that we overcome evil with good.

We remember, but not with any desire for vengeance or as an incentive to hatred. For us, to remember is to pray for peace and justice, and to commit ourselves to their cause. Only a world at peace, with justice for all, can avoid repeating the mistakes and terrible crimes of the past.

As bishop of Rome and successor of the Apostle Peter, I assure the Jewish people that the Catholic Church, motivated by the Gospel law of truth and love, and by no political considerations, is deeply saddened by the hatred, acts of persecution and displays of anti-Semitism directed against the Jews by Christians at any time and in any place.

The church rejects racism in any form as a denial of the image of the Creator inherent in every human being.

In this place of solemn remembrance, I fervently pray that our sorrow for the tragedy which the Jewish people suffered in the 20th century will lead to a new relationship between Christians and Jews. Let us build a new future in which there will be no more anti-Jewish feeling among Christians or anti-Christian feeling among Jews, but rather the mutual respect required of those who adore the one Creator and Lord, and look to Abraham as our common father in faith.

The world must heed the warning that comes to us from the victims of the Holocaust, and from the testimony of the survivors. Here at Yad Vashem the memory lives on, and burns itself onto our souls. It makes us cry out: "I hear the whispering of many - terror on every side - but I trust in you, O Lord: I say, 'You are my God.'"

■

Biographical Sketch: Elizabeth I (September 7, 1533–March 24, 1603) was Queen of England, Queen of France (in name only), and Queen of Ireland from November 17, 1558 until her death. Since she never married, she is sometimes referred to as The Virgin Queen, Gloriana, or Good Queen Bess. She was the sixth and final monarch of the Tudor dynasty. During her reign of over 45 years, there was a marked increase in English power and their influence all over the world. Her period was also marked by great religious turmoil within England.

Elizabeth's reign is referred to as the Elizabethan era or the Golden Age of Elizabeth. Playwrights like William Shakespeare, Christopher Marlowe, and Ben Jonson flourished during this era.

Speech By: Queen Elizabeth I of England

Topic: Speech to the Troops at Tilbury

Date: 1588

My loving people,

We have been persuaded by some that are careful of our safety, to take heed how we commit ourselves to armed multitudes, for fear of treachery; but I assure you I do not desire to live to distrust my faithful and loving people. Let tyrants fear, I have always so behaved myself that, under God, I have placed my chiefest strength and safeguard in the loyal hearts and good-will of my subjects; and therefore I am come amongst you, as you see, at this time, not for my recreation and disport, but being resolved, in the midst and heat of the battle, to live and die amongst you all; to lay down for my God, and for my kingdom, and my people, my honour and my blood, even in the dust. I know I have the body but of a weak and feeble woman; but I have the heart and stomach of a king, and of a king of England too, and think foul scorn that Parma or Spain, or any prince of Europe, should dare to invade the borders of my realm; to which rather than any dishonour shall grow by me, I myself will take up arms, I myself will be your general, judge, and rewarder of every one of your virtues in the field. I know already, for your forwardness you have deserved rewards and crowns; and we do assure you in the word of a prince, they shall be duly paid you. In the mean time, my lieutenant general shall be in my stead, than whom never prince commanded a more noble or worthy subject; not doubting but by your obedience to my general, by your concord in the camp, and your valour in the field, we shall shortly have a famous victory over those enemies of my God, of my kingdom, and of my people.

■

Biographical Sketch: Sir Winston Leonard Spencer-Churchill (November 30, 1874–January 24, 1965) was an English statesman, soldier, author and Prime Minister of the United Kingdom during the Second World War. He is wellknown as an orator, strategist and politician. He was one of the most important leaders in modern British and world history. In 1953, he won the Nobel Prize in Literature for his books on English and world history.

Speeches By: Sir Winston Churchill

Topic: Blood, Toil, Tears and Sweat

Date: May 13, 1940

I beg to move,

That this House welcomes the formation of a Government representing the united and inflexible resolve of the nation to prosecute the war with Germany to a victorious conclusion.

On Friday evening last I received His Majesty's commission to form a new Administration. It as the evident wish and will of Parliament and the nation that this should be conceived on the broadest possible basis and that it should include all parties, both those who supported the late Government and also the parties of the Opposition. I have completed the most important part of this task. A War Cabinet has been formed of five Members, representing, with the Opposition Liberals, the unity of the nation. The three party Leaders have agreed to serve, either in the War Cabinet or in high executive office. The three Fighting Services have been filled. It was necessary that this should be done in one single day, on account of the extreme urgency and rigour of events. A number of other positions, key positions, were filled yesterday, and I am submitting a further list to His Majesty to-night. I hope to complete the appointment of the principal Ministers during to-morrow. The appointment of the other Ministers usually takes a little longer, but I trust that, when Parliament meets again, this part of my task will be completed, and that the administration will be complete in all respects.

I considered it in the public interest to suggest that the House should be summoned to meet today. Mr. Speaker agreed, and took the necessary steps, in accordance with the powers conferred upon him by the Resolution of the House. At the end of the proceedings today, the Adjournment of the House will be proposed until Tuesday, 21st May, with, of course, provision for earlier meeting, if need be. The business to be considered during that week will be notified to Members at the earliest opportunity. I now invite the House, by the Motion which stands in my name, to record its approval of the steps taken and to declare its confidence in the new Government.

To form an administration of this scale and complexity is a serious undertaking in itself, but it must be remembered that we are in the preliminary stage of one of the greatest battles in history, that we are in action at many other points in Norway and in Holland, that we have to be prepared in the Mediterranean, that the air battle is continuous and that many preparations, such as have been indicated by my hon. Friend below the Gangway, have to be made here at home. In this crisis I hope I may be pardoned if I do not address the House at any length today. I hope that any of my friends and colleagues, or former colleagues, who are affected by the political reconstruction, will make allowance, all allowance, for any lack of ceremony with which it has been necessary to act. I would say to the House, as I said to those who have joined this government: "I have nothing to offer but blood, toil, tears and sweat."

We have before us an ordeal of the most grievous kind. We have before us many, many long months of struggle and of suffering. You ask, what is our policy? I can say: It is to wage war, by sea, land and air, with all our might and with all the strength that God can give us; to wage war against a monstrous tyranny, never surpassed in the dark, lamentable catalogue of human crime. That is our policy. You ask, what is our aim? I can answer in one word: It is victory, victory at all costs, victory in spite of all terror, victory, however long and hard the road may be; for without victory, there is no survival. Let that be realised; no survival for the British Empire, no survival for all that the British Empire has stood for, no survival for the urge and impulse of the ages, that mankind will move forward towards its goal. But I take up my task with buoyancy and hope. I feel sure that our cause will not be suffered to fail among men. At this time I feel entitled to claim the aid of all, and I say, "Come then, let us go forward together with our united strength."

★

Second Speech by: Sir Winston Churchill

Topic: Never Give In

Date: October 29, 1941

Almost a year has passed since I came down here at your Head Master's kind invitation in order to cheer myself and cheer the hearts of a few of my friends by singing some of our own songs.

The ten months that have passed have seen very terrible catastrophic events in the world–ups and downs, misfortunes–but can anyone sitting here this afternoon, this October afternoon, not feel deeply thankful for what has happened in the time that has passed and for the very great improvement in the position of our country and of our home?

Why, when I was here last time we were quite alone, desperately alone, and we had been so for five or six months. We were poorly armed. We are not so poorly armed today; but then we were very poorly armed. We had the unmeasured menace of the enemy and their air attack still beating upon us, and you yourselves had had experience of this attack; and I expect you are beginning to feel impatient that there has been this long lull with nothing particular turning up!

But we must learn to be equally good at what is short and sharp and what is long and tough. It is generally said that the British are often better at the last. They do not expect to move from crisis to crisis; they do not always expect that each day will bring up some noble chance of war; but when they very slowly make up their minds that the thing has to be done and the job put through and finished, then, even if it takes months–if it takes years–they do it.

Another lesson I think we may take, just throwing our minds back to our meeting here ten months ago and now, is that appearances are often very deceptive, and as Kipling well says, we must "...meet with Triumph and Disaster. And treat those two impostors just the same."

You cannot tell from appearances how things will go. Sometimes imagination makes things out far worse than they are; yet without imagination not much can be done. Those people who are imaginative see many more dangers than perhaps exist; certainly many more than will happen; but then they must also pray to be given that extra courage to carry this far-reaching imagination.

But for everyone, surely, what we have gone through in this period–I am addressing myself to the School–surely from this period of ten months, this is the lesson:

Never give in. Never give in. Never, never, never, never–in nothing, great or small, large or petty–never give in, except to convictions of honor and good sense. Never yield to force. Never yield to the apparently overwhelming might of the enemy.

We stood all alone a year ago, and to many countries it seemed that our account was closed, we were finished. All this tradition of ours, our songs, our School history, this part of the history of this country, were gone and finished and liquidated.

Very different is the mood today. Britain, other nations thought, had drawn a sponge across her slate. But instead our country stood in the gap. There was no flinching and no thought of giving in; and by what seemed almost a miracle to those outside these Islands, though we ourselves never doubted it, we now find ourselves in a position where I say that we can be sure that we have only to persevere to conquer.

You sang here a verse of a School Song: you sang that extra verse written in my honour, which I was very greatly complimented by and which you have repeated today. But there is one word in it I want to alter–I wanted to do so last year, but I did not venture to. It is the line: "Not less we praise in darker days."

I have obtained the Head Master's permission to alter darker to sterner. "Not less we praise in sterner days."

Do not let us speak of darker days: let us speak rather of sterner days. These are not dark days; these are great days–the greatest days our country has ever lived; and we must all thank God that we have been allowed, each of us according to our stations, to play a part in making these days memorable in the history of our race.

■

Biographical Sketch: Subhash Chandra Bose (January 23, 1897–August 18, 1945) was one of the most prominent leaders of the Indian Independence Movement against the British Rule. Popular as Netaji, he was a prominent supporter of the Axis as a counterweight to European imperialism during the Second World War. He was elected president of the Indian National Congress for two consecutive terms. However, he had to resign from the post in the face of a motion of no-confidence, due to his ideological conflicts with Mahatma Gandhi. He felt that Mahatma Gandhi's non-violence strategy would not be sufficient to secure India's independence. He advocated violent resistance and established a separate political party, the All India Forward Bloc and called for full and immediate independence of India from British rule.

Speech By: Subhash Chandra Bose

Topic: Give Me Blood! I Promise You Freedom!!

Date: July 4, 1944 at a rally of Indians in Burma

Friends! Twelve months ago a new programme of 'total mobilisation' or 'maximum sacrifice' was placed before Indians in East Asia. Today I shall give you an account of our achievements during the past year and shall place before you our demands for the coming year. But, before I do so, I want you to realise once again what a golden opportunity we have for winning freedom. The British are engaged in a worldwide struggle and in the course of this struggle they have suffered defeat after defeat on so many fronts. The enemy having been thus considerably weakened, our fight for liberty has become very much easier than it was five years ago. Such a rare and God-given opportunity comes once in a century. That is why we have sworn to fully utilise this opportunity for liberating our motherland from the British yoke.

I am so very hopeful and optimistic about the outcome of our struggle, because I do not rely merely on the efforts of three million Indians in East Asia. There is a gigantic movement going on inside India and millions of our countrymen are prepared for maximum suffering and sacrifice in order to achieve liberty.

Unfortunately, ever since the great fight of 1857, our countrymen are disarmed, whereas the enemy is armed to the teeth. Without arms and without a modern army, it is impossible for a disarmed people to win freedom in this modern age. Through the grace of Providence and through the help of generous Nippon, it has become possible for Indians in East Asia to get arms to build up a modern army. Moreover, Indians in East Asia are united to a man in the endeavour to win freedom and all the religious and other differences that the British tried to engineer inside India, simply do not exist in East Asia. Consequently, we have now an ideal combination of circumstances favouring the success of our struggle- and all that is wanted is that Indians should themselves come forward to pay the price of liberty. According to the programme of 'total mobilisation', I demanded of you men, money and materials. Regarding men, I am glad to tell you that I have obtained sufficient recruits already. Recruits have come to us from every corner of East Asia–from China, Japan, Indo-China, Philippines, Java, Borneo, Celebes, Sumatra, Malaya, Thailand and Burma.

You must continue the mobilisation of men, money and materials with greater vigour and energy, in particular, the problem of supplies and transport has to be solved satisfactorily.

We require more men and women of all categories for

administration and reconstruction in liberated areas. We must be prepared for a situation in which the enemy will ruthlessly apply the scorched earth policy, before withdrawing from a particular area and will also force the civilian population to evacuate as was attempted in Burma.

The most important of all is the problem of sending reinforcements in men and in supplies to the fighting fronts. If we do not do so, we cannot hope to maintain our success at the fronts. Nor can we hope to penetrate deeper into India.

Those of you who will continue to work on the Home Front should never forget that East Asia–and particularly Burma–from our base for the war of liberation. If this base is not strong, our fighting forces can never be victorious. Remember that this is a 'total war'–and not merely a war between two armies. That is why for a full one year I have been laying so much stress on 'total mobilisation' in the East.

There is another reason why I want you to look after the Home Front properly. During the coming months I and my colleagues on the War Committee of the Cabinet desire to devote our whole attention to the fighting front- and also to the task of working up the revolution inside India. Consequently, we want to be fully assured that the work at the base will go on smoothly and uninterruptedly even in our absence.

Friends, one year ago, when I made certain demands of you, I told you that if you give me 'total mobilisation', I would give you a 'second front'. I have redeemed that pledge. The first phase of our campaign is over. Our victorious troops, fighting side by side with Nipponese troops, have pushed back the enemy and are now fighting bravely on the sacred soil of our dear motherland.

Gird up your loins for the task that now lies ahead. I had asked you for men, money and materials. I have got them in generous measure. Now I demand more of you. Men, money and materials cannot by themselves bring victory or freedom. We must have the motive-power that will inspire us to brave deeds and heroic exploits.

It will be a fatal mistake for you to wish to live and see India free simply because victory is now within reach. No one here should have the desire to live to enjoy freedom. A long fight is still in front of us.

We should have but one desire today–the desire to die so that India may live–the desire to face a martyr's death, so that the path to freedom may be paved with the martyr's blood.

Friend's! My comrades in the War of Liberation! Today I demand of you one thing, above all. I demand of you blood. It is blood alone that can avenge the blood that the enemy has spilt. It is blood alone that can pay the price of freedom. *Give me blood and I promise you freedom!*

■

Biographical Sketch: Tim Collins is a former colonel in the British Army. He is best known for his role in the Iraq War 2003. As Lieutenant Colonel of the 1st Battalion, Royal Irish Regiment of the British Army, he gave a rousing eve-of-battle speech to his troops in Iraq. The speech was extemporised, and was recorded in shorthand by a single journalist. It is said that US President George W Bush subsequently had a copy of the speech tacked up on the wall of the Oval Office. Commentators claim to have detected a number of Biblical and Shakespearian influences in the speech.

Speech By: Tim Collins

Topic: Eve-of-battle Speech

Date: March 19, 2003

We go to liberate, not to conquer.

We will not fly our flags in their country.

We are entering Iraq to free a people and the only flag which will be flown in that ancient land is their own. Show respect for them.

There are some who are alive at this moment who will not be alive shortly. Those who do not wish to go on that journey, we will not send. As for the others, I expect you to rock their world. Wipe them out if that is what they choose. But if you are ferocious in battle remember to be magnanimous in victory.

Iraq is steeped in history.

It is the site of the Garden of Eden, of the Great Flood and the birthplace of Abraham.

Tread lightly there.

You will see things that no man could pay to see–and you will have to go a long way to find a more decent, generous and upright people than the Iraqis. You will be embarrassed by their hospitality even though they have nothing.

Don't treat them as refugees for they are in their own country. Their children will be poor, in years to come they will know that the light of liberation in their lives was brought by you.

If there are casualties of war then remember that when they woke up and got dressed in the morning they did not plan to die this day.

Allow them dignity in death.

Bury them properly and mark their graves.

It is my foremost intention to bring every single one of you out alive.

But there may be people among us who will not see the end of this campaign.

We will put them in their sleeping bags and send them back.

There will be no time for sorrow.

The enemy should be in no doubt that we are his nemesis and that we are bringing about his rightful destruction. There are many regional commanders who have stains on their souls and they are stoking the fires of hell for Saddam. He and his forces will be destroyed by this coalition for what they have done. As they die they will know their deeds have brought them to this place. Show them no pity.

It is a big step to take another human life.

It is not to be done lightly.

I know of men who have taken life needlessly in other conflicts.

I can assure you they live with the mark of Cain upon them.

If someone surrenders to you then remember they have that right in international law and ensure that one day they go home to their family. The ones who wish to fight, well, we aim to please.

If you harm the regiment or its history by over-enthusiasm in killing or in cowardice, know it is your family who will suffer. You will be shunned unless your conduct is of the highest–for your deeds will follow you down through history. We will bring shame on neither our uniform nor our nation.

(On Saddam's chemical and biological weapons.)

It is not a question of if, it's a question of when. We know he has already devolved the decision to lower commanders, and that means he has already taken the decision himself. If we survive the first strike we will survive the attack.

As for ourselves, let's bring everyone home and leave Iraq a better place for us having been there.

Our business now is north.

■

Biographical Sketch: Narendra Damodardas Modi born 17 September 1950 is an Indian politician serving as the 14th and current Prime Minister of India since 2014. He was the Chief Minister of Gujarat from 2001 to 2014, and is the Member of Parliament for Varanasi. Modi, a member of the Bharatiya Janata Party (BJP), is a Hindu nationalist and member of the right-wing Rashtriya Swayamsevak Sangh (RSS).

Speech By: Narender Modi

Topic: Independent Day of India from Red Fort

Date: August 15, 2014

My dear fellow citizens,

Greetings from the ramparts of the Red Fort on the auspicious occasion of Independence Day.

Nation is celebrating the Independence Day with the festival of Janamashtmi today . I can see a number of Bal Kanahiyas here. We are fortunate to have in our cultural and historical heritage from a Sudarshan Chakradhari Mohan to Charkhadhari Mohan.

From the ramparts of Red Fort, on behalf of our 125 crore countrymen, I bow and pay respects to all those men and women who have sacrificed their lives, who have undergone immense sufferings and made sacrifices for the independence, glory and pride of the country.

Sometimes, natural calamities are a big challenge for us. A good monsoon contributes immensely to the prosperity of the country. However, due to climate change, sometimes it turns into a natural calamity. Several parts of the country faced natural calamities recently. Besides our innocent children lost their lives in a hospital. Our 125 crore countrymen stand shoulder to shoulder with them in this hour of crisis and grief. I assure the countrymen that in this hour of crisis we shall leave no stone unturned to ensure the wellbeing of all.

My dear countrymen, this year is a special year for independent India. We commemorated 75 years of Quit India Movement last week. This year we are also commemorating the centenary of Champaran Satyagrah and the Sabarmati Ashram. The centenary of Lokmanya Tilak's call "Swaraj is my birth right" falls this year as well. The year marks the 125th Anniversary of the Ganesh Utsav which led to the rise of community awakening through the celebrations. It inspires us to dedicate ourselves to a cause for the country. A collective resolve of the citizens was visible during 1942 to 1947 across the country which forced the British to Quit India within a span of five years. We will have to exhibit the same resolve from now on in the 70th year of independence to 2022, the 75th year of independence.

We now have five years before we reach the 75th year of our independence. Our united resolve, strength and determination to work hard remembering the memory of our great patriots will help us to build an India of their dreams by 2022. Therefore, we have to take the country forward with a pledge to build a New India.

We are aware of the power of the collective resolve, hard work, sacrifice and devotion of our 125 crore citizens. Lord Krishna was immensely powerful, but it is only when the milkmen came out with sticks in his support that they could lift the Govardhan parvat. When Lord Rama had to go to Lanka, the monkeys of vanar sena came to his help, Ramsetu was built and Lord Rama could reach Lanka. Then there was Mohandas Karamchand Gandhi, who empowered his countrymen to weave the fabric of independence with cotton and spinning wheel.

The collective resolve and strength of the people got freedom for our country. No one is small or big. We have in our memory the story of squirrel which became an agent of change. That's why we must remember that no one among the 1.25 billion people is either small or big – everyone is equal.

If each one of us, irrespective of where he belongs to, strives with a new resolve, a new energy, a new strength, we can change the face of the country with our combined strength in the 75th year of our independence in 2022. It will be the New India – a secure, prosperous and strong nation. A New India where there is equal opportunity for all; where modern science and technology play an important role in bringing glory for the nation in the global arena.

Our freedom movement is linked to our sentiments. We know it well that at the time of the freedom movement, the teacher who was engaged in teaching, the farmer who was tilling his land, the laborer who was working – all of them knew in their hearts that whatever they were doing, was contributing towards the independence of the country. This idea is a great source of strength. In the family, food is prepared everyday but it becomes 'prasad' only when it is offered to the deity.

We are working, but if we do so in the spirit of working for the glory of mother India, for the divinity of mother India, if we do it to rid our countrymen of poverty, if we do it to properly weave our social fabric, if we discharge our duties with feelings towards the country, if we do it with a sense of devotion to country, if we do our work by dedicating it to the country, then the achievements will be much more. That is why we should move forward with this spirit.

January 1, 2018 will not be an ordinary day – those born in this century will start turning 18. For these people, this is a decisive year of their lives. They are going to be the creator of the destiny (Bhagya Vidhata) of our nation in the 21st century. I heartily welcome all these youth, honour them and offer my respects to them. You have an opportunity to shape the destiny of our country. A proud nation invites you to become a part of its developmental journey.

■

Biographical Sketch: Donald John Trump (born June 14, 1946) is the 45th and current President of the United States, in office since January 20, 2017. Before entering politics, he was a businessman and television personality.

Trump was born and raised in the New York City borough of Queens, and received an economics degree from the Wharton School of the University of Pennsylvania. Trump co-authored several books, including The Art of the Deal. He owned the Miss Universe and Miss USA beauty pageants from 1996 to 2015.

Speech By: Donald Trump

Topic: American Carnage

Date: January 17, 2017

Chief Justice Roberts, President Carter, President Clinton, President Bush, President Obama, fellow Americans, and people of the world: thank you.

We, the citizens of America, are now joined in a great national effort to rebuild our country and restore its promise for all of our people.

Together, we will determine the course of America and the world for many, many years to come.

We will face challenges. We will confront hardships. But we will get the job done.

Every four years, we gather on these steps to carry out the orderly and peaceful transfer of power, and we are grateful to President Obama and First Lady Michelle Obama for their gracious aid throughout this transition. They have been magnificent. Thank you.

Today's ceremony, however, has very special meaning. Because today we are not merely transferring power from one Administration to another, or from one party to another – but we are transferring power from Washington DC and giving it back to you, the people.

For too long, a small group in our nation's Capital has reaped the rewards of government while the people have borne the cost.

Washington flourished – but the people did not share in its wealth.

Politicians prospered – but the jobs left, and the factories closed.

The establishment protected itself, but not the citizens of our country.

Their victories have not been your victories; their triumphs have not been your triumphs; and while they celebrated in our nation's capital, there was little to celebrate for struggling families all across our land.

That all changes – starting right here, and right now, because this moment is your moment: it belongs to you.

It belongs to everyone gathered here today and everyone watching all across America.

This is your day. This is your celebration.

And this, the United States of America, is your country.

What truly matters is not which party controls our government, but whether our government is controlled by the people.

January 20, 2017, will be remembered as the day the people became the rulers of this nation again.

The forgotten men and women of our country will be forgotten no longer.

Everyone is listening to you now.

You came by the tens of millions to become part of a historic movement the likes of which the world has never seen before.

At the center of this movement is a crucial conviction: that a nation exists to serve its citizens.

Americans want great schools for their children, safe neighborhoods for their families, and good jobs for themselves.

These are just and reasonable demands of righteous people and a righteous public.

But for too many of our citizens, a different reality exists: mothers and children trapped in poverty in our inner cities; rusted-out factories scattered like tombstones across the landscape of our nation; an education system, flush with cash, but which leaves our young and beautiful students deprived of all knowledge; and the crime and the gangs and the drugs that have stolen too many lives and robbed our country of so much unrealized potential.

This American carnage stops right here and stops right now.

We are one nation – and their pain is our pain. Their dreams are our dreams; and their success will be our success. We share one heart, one home, and one glorious destiny.

The oath of office I take today is an oath of allegiance to all Americans.

For many decades, we've enriched foreign industry at the expense of American industry; subsidized the armies of other countries while allowing for the very sad depletion of our military; we've defended other nations' borders while refusing to defend our own; and spent trillions and trillions of dollars overseas while America's infrastructure has fallen into disrepair and decay.

We've made other countries rich while the wealth, strength, and confidence of our country has dissipated over the horizon.

One by one, the factories shuttered and left our shores, with not even a thought about the millions and millions of American workers that were left behind

The wealth of our middle class has been ripped from their homes and then redistributed all across the world.

But that is the past. And now we are looking only to the future.

We assembled here today are issuing a new decree to be heard in every city, in every foreign capital, and in every hall of power.

From this day forward, a new vision will govern our land.

From this day forward, it's going to be only America first, America first.

Every decision on trade, on taxes, on immigration, on foreign affairs, will be made to benefit American workers and American families.

We must protect our borders from the ravages of other countries making our products, stealing our companies, and destroying our jobs. Protection will lead to great prosperity and strength.

I will fight for you with every breath in my body – and I will never, ever let you down.

So to all Americans, in every city near and far, small and large, from mountain to mountain, and from ocean to ocean, hear these words:

You will never be ignored again.

Your voice, your hopes, and your dreams, will define our American destiny. And your courage and goodness and love will forever guide us along the way.

Together, we will make America strong again.

We will make America wealthy again.

We will make America proud again.

We will make America safe again.

And, yes, together, we will make America great again. Thank you, God bless you, and God bless America.

■

Biographical Sketch: Vladimir Vladimirovich Putin born 7 October 1952 is a Russian politician serving as the current President of Russia since 7 May 2012, previously holding the position from 2000 until 2008. He was Prime Minister of Russia from 1999 until the beginning of his first presidency in 2000, and again between presidencies from 2008 until 2012. During his first term as Prime Minister, he served as Acting President of Russia due to the resignation of President Boris Yeltsin. During his second term as Prime Minister, he was the chairman of the ruling United Russia party.

Speech By: Valdimir Putin

Topic: Presidential Address to the Federal Assembly

Date: March 1, 2018

Citizens of Russia, members of the Federation Council and State Duma,

Today's Address is a very special landmark event, just as the times we are living in, when the choices we make and every step we take are set to shape the future of our country for decades to come.

It is at such turning points that Russia has proven, time and again, its ability to develop and renew itself, discover new territories, build cities, conquer space and make major discoveries. This unwavering forward-looking drive, coupled with traditions and values, ensured the continuity in the thousand-year-long history of our nation.

We have gone through major challenging transformations, and were able to overcome new and extremely complex economic and social challenges, preserved the unity of our country, built a democratic society and set it on the path to freedom and independence.

We ensured sustainability and stability in almost all areas of life, which is critical for a huge and multi-ethnic country like ours with its complex federative structure and diversity of cultures, with historical divides that are still alive in people's memory and major challenges Russia had to face over the course of its history.

Before the Presidential Address to the Federal Assembly.

However, sustainability is the foundation of development but not its guarantee. We have no right to allow a situation when the stability that has been achieved would lead to complacency, all the more so as many problems remain unresolved.

Today, Russia ranks among the world's leading nations with a powerful foreign economic and defence potential. But we have not yet reached the required level in the context of accomplishing our highly important task and guaranteeing people's quality of life and prosperity. But we must do this, and we will do this.

As I said in the past, the state's role and positions in the modern world are not determined only or predominantly by natural resources or production capacities; the decisive role is played by the people, as well as conditions for every individual's development, self-assertion and creativity. Therefore, everything hinges on efforts to preserve the people of Russia and to guarantee the prosperity of our citizens We must achieve a decisive breakthrough in this area.

I repeat, a solid foundation has been created for this. Therefore, we can now set and accomplish new tasks. We already have substantial experience in implementing ambitious programmes and social projects. The Russian economy has proved its resilience, and the current stable macro-economic situation opens up new opportunities for surging ahead and maintaining long-term growth.

Finally, the world is now accumulating a tremendous technological potential making it possible to achieve a real breakthrough in improving the people's quality of life and modernising the economy, the infrastructure and state governance and administration. How effectively we will able to use the colossal potentialities of the technological revolution, and how we will respond to its challenges depends on us alone. In this sense, the next few years will prove decisive for the country's future. I reiterate, these years will be decisive.

I will tell you why. What I will say now has no connection to the domestic political cycle or even the presidential election. No matter who is elected President, each Russian citizen and all of us together must be able to see what is going on in the world, what is happening around us, and what challenges we are facing.

The speed of technological progress is accelerating sharply. It is rising dramatically. Those who manage to ride this technological wave will surge far ahead. Those who fail to do this will be submerged and drown in this wave.

Technological lag and dependence translate into reduced security and economic opportunities of the country and, ultimately, the loss of its sovereignty. This is the way things stand now. The lag inevitably weakens and erodes the human potential. Because new jobs, modern companies and an attractive life will develop in other, more successful countries where educated and talented young people will go, thereby draining the society's vital powers and development energy.

As I have said, changes concern the entire civilization, and the sheer scale of these changes calls for an equally powerful response.

We are ready to provide it. We are ready for a genuine breakthrough.

My confidence is based on the results we have achieved together, even though they may seem modest at first glance, as well as on the unity of Russian society and, most importantly, on the huge potential of Russia and our talented and ingenious people.

In order to move forward and to develop dynamically, we must expand freedom in all spheres, strengthen democratic institutions, local governments, civil society institutions and courts, and also open the country to the world and to new ideas and initiatives.

It is high time we take a number of tough decisions that are long overdue. We need to get rid of anything that stands in the way of our development and prevents people from fully unleashing their potential. It is our obligation to focus all resources and summon all our strength and willpower in this daring effort that must yield results.

Otherwise, there will be no future for us, our children or our country. It is not a question of someone conquering or devastating our land. No, that is not the danger. The main threat and our main enemy is the fact that we are falling behind. If we are unable to reverse this trend, we will fall even further behind. This is like a serious chronic disease that steadily saps the energy from the body and destroys it from within step by step. Quite often, this destructive process goes unnoticed by the body.

We need to master creative power and boost development so that no obstacles prevent us from moving forward with confidence and independently. We must take ownership of our destiny.

■

Other Books on
GENERAL SERIES

1. Chanakya Neeti **(New)**
2. Helpline for Stressed Parents **(New)**
3. Grow Rich with Peace of Mind **(New)**
4. How to be Fit and Young **(New)**
5. How to Succeed in Life **(New)**
6. 100 Ways to Develop Self Confidence
7. Child Development
8. Abraham Lincoln A Complete Biography
9. Mein Kampf My Struggle
10. Think and Grow Rich
11. The Art of Personality Development
12. Positive Mind Power
13. Travel & Tourism An Industry Facilitator
14. World's Great Authors And Poets
15. Effective Editing Help Yourself in Becoming a Good Editor
16. Smart House-Keeping for Modern Women
17. Develop Super Power Memory
18. World's Great Personalities
19. Personality Plus
20. Power of Positive Thinking
21. Art of Successful Parenting
22. A Handbook of Etiquettes
23. World's Great Scientists
24. Body Language

25. Art of Successful Living
26. Jokes for All
27. Selected Dohas
28. Baby Names for Girls **(New)**
29. Baby Names for Boys **(New)**
30. Art of Public Speaking
31. The World's Greatest Speeches
32. Group Discussions
33. Personality Development
34. Think Positive & Things Will Go Right
35. Once in a Blue Moon (A Tantra Tale)
36. God is Dead
37. Travel India (A Complete Guide for Tourists)
38. Glimpses of Urdu Poetry
39. How to Reduce Tension
40. A Book of Stenography
41. Baby Names for the Boy
42. Baby Names for the Girl
43. Ripples in Tranquil Waters

Lotus PRESS

Unit No. 220, 2nd Floor, 4735/22, Prakash Deep Building,
Ansari Road, Darya Ganj, New Delhi- 110002
Ph.: 41325510, 98118-38000
E-mail : lotuspress1984@gmail.com, www.lotuspress.co.in